CONTENTS

DECISION POWER
How to Make Successful Decisions with Confidence

Harvey Kaye

PRENTICE HALL
Englewood Cliffs, New Jersey 07632

Prentice-Hall International (UK) Limited, *London*
Prentice-Hall of Australia Pty. Limited, *Sydney*
Prentice-Hall Canada, Inc., *Toronto*
Prentice-Hall Hispanoamericana, S.A., *Mexico*
Prentice-Hall of India Private Limited, *New Delhi*
Prentice-Hall of Japan, Inc., *Tokyo*
Simon & Schuster Asia Pte. Ltd., *Singapore*
Editora Prentice-Hall do Brasil, Ltda., *Rio de Janeiro*

10 9 8 7 6 5 4 3 2

To Kathleen

Library of Congress Cataloging-in-Publication Data

Kaye, Harvey.
   Decision Power : how to make successful decisions with confidence
by Harvey Kaye.
      p. cm.

Includes bibliographical references and index.
   ISBN 0-13-203530-8 (case) ISBN 0-13-203548-0 (pbk.) :
   1. Decision-making. 2. Problem solving—Psychological aspects.
I. Title.
BF448.K38 1992
153.8'3—dc20   91-45549
                                                                     CIP

ISBN 0-13-203530-8

ISBN 0-13-203548-0 PBK

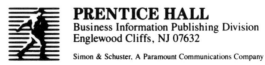

PRENTICE HALL
Business Information Publishing Division
Englewood Cliffs, NJ 07632

Simon & Schuster, A Paramount Communications Company

Printed in the United States of America

7. SEIZE OPPORTUNITIES 91

8. GAIN SUPPORT FOR YOUR DECISIONS 105

9. CONQUER WISHFUL THINKING 119

10. MANAGE SETBACKS AND UNCERTAINTY 139

INTRODUCTION

THE SIGNIFICANCE OF DECISIONS
IN EVERYDAY LIFE

If you've picked up this book, chances are that something in your life desperately needs changing, but so far you haven't come up with any good answers. Perhaps it's a health problem, an unsatisfactory job, a bad marriage, a financial dilemma, a midlife career crisis, or a vague desire to live a more spiritual life-style. Whatever it may be, a question has been rolling around in your head for some time: "What should I do?"

The purpose of this book is to make you less fearful of making major decisions. It will show you how to cut big decisions down to size. You will learn how to *think* and *feel* about your problem in useful ways. Each of the twelve chapters presents an invaluable decision-making tool. Used together, they form a tool kit that prepares you for a wide variety of decision-making challenges. In particular, you will see how to:

- Define the problem in a productive way

- Visualize new goals

- Accept the challenge and risk of change

- Structure your efforts

- Access your resources

- Exercise better judgment in choosing among alternatives

- Overcome obstacles that stand in your way

- Accept responsibility for your own future

- Make trade-offs when your secondary goals conflict with your primary ones

- Overcome inertia and procrastination

- Reality-test your decisions

- Use knowledge of your likes and limitations to your own benefit

- Manage postdecision regret by preparing yourself for possible setbacks or momentary reverses

- Develop confidence and courage

Decision making is not something you can avoid. Unless your every thought, motion, and desire are magically controlled by another person, you'll have to make your own decisions to find suitable work, a mate, rewarding personal relationships, satisfying recreation, physical health, spiritual inspiration, and emotional well-being.

Your decisions define you. They reflect your unique set of values, goals, and aspirations. Don't become one of those people who cops out of effective decisions by:

1. Choosing the first available option impulsively (hoping luck will see you through)

2. Letting others decide for you (abdicating your personal responsibility)

3. Waiting (hoping that the problem will go away or that fate will magically bring you the things you need)

SUBSTANCE VERSUS ILLUSION
IN DECISION MAKING

> . . . one of the major functions of consciousness [is] to decide and to will. The greater the realm of consciousness, the greater the realm of choice. The greater the realm of unconsciousness, the smaller the area in which man can exert his will.
>
> Silvano Arieti[1]

This book gives many methods that you can apply to your everyday decisions. But it does not stop there. It also invites you to become more perceptive about your own thoughts, feelings, and values. That is, it encourages you to discover what your values are, how you *feel* about the problem, and how to sharpen your thinking and logic in solving the problem. It is hoped that you will come closer to self-knowledge. In Arieti's terms, this book helps you increase the realm of your choices by increasing the realm of your consciousness.

Now this is no small feat, for it's all too easy to go through the motions of decision making without really being committed to the required action. It's quite possible to fool yourself into thinking that you have made an effective decision, whereas all you have done is construct a more subtle cover-up for an underlying desire to avoid something fearful or anxiety producing.

Many years ago, I fooled myself with this very technique. I faced a tough career choice. At the time, I had read a few books on the quantitative decision-making methods used in science and business. These methods, developed for business problems with many contributing factors, were ideal to sort out the various considerations and give an overall judgment about the best course of action. To do this, each criterion (against which the options are to be measured) is given a numerical weight. Each option is then scored for all the criteria. The option with the highest score is the best bet.

I followed the prescribed formulas zealously. I prepared a ten-page analysis that indicated one option was clearly the

---

[1] *The Will to Be Human* (1972) New York: Quadrangle Books, Inc., p. 44.

best. . . . I chose it. Three months later, I realized that I had made a mistake. Somehow, I had fooled myself. I had misused the method. For, although I had many options available to me, I prematurely turned the decision process into "Pick either option A or option B." Yet neither option really satisfied the problem because both failed to address my underlying needs. I didn't consider alternatives other than those two because I was afraid of the large changes they might require. Further, I acted against my own best interest by disallowing viable options that would have simply required marketing myself more aggressively.

By limiting my alternatives to only those two, I was able to hide from my fears. I fooled myself into thinking that I was putting well-considered effort into my choice. In retrospect, both options were acceptable on the outside, but were inappropriate from an inner criterion. They may have been adequate for *some* people in my situation, but not for *me*.

By limiting my alternatives, I was able to hide from my fears.

In short, I had not included my own values into the decision. I looked at salary, benefits, status, commuting distance, and the future growth of the employer, but had ignored whether the jobs offered any real match to my goals and values. Further, I paid too much attention to how much each prospective employer wanted me. When they took me out to a fancy restaurant for the "human relations" part of the interview, I was paying more attention to how much money they were spending on me than on whom I would be working with. I never asked myself, "How much do *I* want *them*?"

Because it is so easy to deceive yourself in making big decisions, I place heavy emphasis in this book on the psychological underpinnings of decisions. Understanding the telltale signs of self-deception results in better and more fulfilling choices.

REAL DECISIONS REQUIRE BOTH
MIND AND HEART

Why is decision making so hard? Because decisions deal with changes that count, with stakes that are high. We're fearful that a wrong step may hurt us greatly. Problem solving, which is often confused with decision making, is not exactly the same thing. Problem solving can exist in abstract form, separate from the person performing the activity. In algebra, for example, there is a problem and there is a solution, but they are not necessarily *our* problem and *our* solution.

Problem solving is taught in many forms in school. Physics and geometry, for example, are basically problem-solving tools. Their methods allow you to analyze entire classes of problems, reason about the options, and then come up with useful answers.

In practice, many "decisions" fall into the category of problem solving: Given an objective situation—and a few simple goals—some alternatives will emerge as clearly superior to the others. Many business and scientific decision makers utilize these objective tools to analyze the facts and produce an optimal solution.

For example, if you ask ten different business experts to make a complex decision about how many units should be manufactured (given last year's sales figures, warehousing requirements, projections of future sales, cost of materials, cost of capital, and the same rules about maximizing profit and staying within the bounds of the law), their results will be remarkably uniform. Each expert may have a computer program that weighs certain of the factors differently, but their overall decisions will be very similar.

Problem solving is more limited than decision making inasmuch as it is a purely conceptual activity. It emphasizes the rational means to devise options (potential solutions) and then test them mentally (or "on paper") to see if they work. Problem solving requires you to look at the raw data, analyze it, and then devise ways to reach your goal. Yet, problem solving does not define what the problem is in the first place. Each one of us has particular needs, desires, and situations. What is a problem for you may not be a problem for me. As a decision maker, you will also need to access your emotions, become aware of your needs, and make value judgments. All these activities transcend the realm of problem solving.

Because problem solving emphasizes thought over action, it ignores the whole issue of *performance*. As behavioral psychologists have long pointed out, even the best theoretical solutions require effort, risk, and skill to implement. Without the capability to carry out the recommended actions, nothing useful will come of it.

Thus, decision making goes beyond traditional problem solving. Whereas problem solving does not involve a person's sense of self, in decision making, the emotional aspects cannot be separated from the individual. In his philosophical study of decision making, *Freedom and Nature,* (see Suggested Reading List) Paul Ricoeur puts it this way: "In deciding, I impute myself into the world."

You may be wondering by now, "Can decision making be taught, just as algebra?" The answer is, "Yes, but it's more of an art." The methods of instruction are subtle and indirect, but they can be stated nevertheless. This book attempts to do exactly that. The important difference is that decision making involves an emotional aspect that centers on how you, as a unique individual, feel about certain aspects of your own life. It deals with your openness to risk, your acceptance of failure, the strength of your desires, and the sense of self-esteem that you bring to the process.

Instead of teaching you abstract methods, decision-making instruction teaches you how to balance, like riding a bicycle. The measure of success is not a single factor, such as the maximum speed you can attain, but how well balanced you are, considering your manifold goals, limitations, the amount of risk you can handle, and the influences acting on you as a person at that time.

The emotional aspect of decision making focuses on accessing self-knowledge, self-expression, courage, willingness to experiment, overcoming obstacles—and when this cannot be done—accepting limitations. Confidence and self-esteem are established not as *ideas*, but by experiencing ourselves as capable in an ever-expanding sphere of influence. No amount of rational thought alone will move us to make a major commitment. We also need the emotional resources behind the rational thought. Real decisions carry the full weight of our convictions; we make them because they *matter* to us. Real decisions make a difference in our lives. We are willing to endure the costs they entail exactly because they bring benefits that we need and desire.

Real decisions carry the full weight of our convictions; we make them because they *matter* to us.

HOW THIS BOOK CAN HELP YOU MAKE BETTER DECISIONS

This book places equal emphasis on the rational and the emotional aspects of decision making. Without understanding the emotional part of decision making, the thought processes you use to select your goals may have a hidden flaw: The goals may relate more to your fears than to the positive factors that will make you happy.

The emotional part of decision making assures that your goals support your values and satisfy your needs for relatedness, instead of feeding neurotic needs developing from deep-seated insecurities. Such neurotic needs would not make you one whit happier if you were ever able to satisfy them.

On the other hand, without a certain amount of rational problem solving and planning, you may be unable to carry out or sustain your decisions, no matter how well attuned they are to your feelings. The structure and efficiency provided by the rational method enhances the total decision process. Like a scientist, you'll be able to consider the experiences you already possess as *experiments* that provide you with valuable information about your abilities, preferences, and values. You can then modify the experiment to take new conditions into account, and even make educated guesses about how to overcome obstacles as they arise. At each step, your confidence increases as you improve the quality of your judgment and exercise your own initiative.

Chapters 1–6 of *Decision Power* explain the rational aspect of decision making. In particular, Chapter 1 talks about decision anxiety and sorting out the valuable messages that it contains. Chapter 2 helps you to define the problem so that it addresses the real issues. It presents ways to formulate your decision as a problem that can be structured and organized. You'll see that a decision defined in this way has a much higher chance of succeeding.

Chapter 3 shows how to generate alternatives. You'll see that your own decision making "style" may be affecting the way you devise alternatives. Simple ways to compensate for your own style and to develop more alternatives are presented. Chapter 4 discusses ways to evaluate your alternatives. You'll learn how to set criteria by which to judge them, how to use decision trees to clarify your thinking about the possible outcomes, and how to make trade-offs in cases where you must choose between two or more goals pulling you in different directions.

Chapter 5 considers how to overcome obstacles. It shows you ways to look at the obstacles rather than avoid them, thereby allowing you to use the full power of your mind to *divide and conquer*. Chapter 6 is a lesson on planning for the success of your decision. It will help you organize your efforts and coordinate with others for the resources you need.

The art of evaluating opportunities is described in Chapter 7. Opportunities are useful because they complement your long-term plans, but how do you recognize them? Chapter 7 gives practical rules of thumb for seeking and judging fruitful opportunities without wastefully turning each one into a major research project. I describe my unique "flea market model" to develop the concepts needed to evaluate opportunities efficiently.

The emotional aspects of decision making are introduced in Chapters 8–12. You will learn specific skills that are not addressed by the problem-solving approach. You'll see how to access feelings about your goals, how not to deceive yourself with wishful thinking, how to deal with anxiety and confusion, how to handle the impulse to instantly escape a bad situation, how to overcome obstacles that seem overwhelming and unyielding, and how to sustain your decision in the face of setbacks.

Chapter 8 gives invaluable advice on gaining support for your decisions. You'll see why support—from family, friends, coworkers, experts, and others—is absolutely necessary and why you should expect to give something of value in order to get it.

Each one of us draws on the environment for the support we need. As small infants, we counted on our parents to provide for our needs automatically. Now that we are adults, we must make demands (i.e., state needs) because the environment will no longer *anticipate* our needs.

Stating your needs is not sufficient, however. You must also know *how* to satisfy them (that is, how to extract nourishment from the environment). A plant "knows" how to extract nutrients from the soil. Humans do the same thing by making valid *trades*. You learn how to barter for the things you need. To satisfy your needs, you must become adept at motivating others to enter the barter. You must learn how to develop a steady stream of commerce in which the trades are mutually satisfying. Part of the ability to do this comes from an inner feeling of self-worth, from the feeling that (at least) some people in the environment will value what we have to offer.

Judgment in assessing both your own abilities and the nature of external situations is critical to good decision making. Chapter 9 urges you to learn what actions in the decision are within your power to realize. It guides you to perceive your circumstances clearly by not confusing wish for fact, someone else's situation for your own, or what *was* true in the past for what *is* true in the present. Self-trust is an important factor here because there is usually never enough information (before actually implementing the actions) to *guarantee* a result. You must have a certain amount of faith in yourself, in your abilities to carry out your intentions, and in the validity of your perceptions.

Chapter 9 provides a minilesson on developing better judgment. It explains how certain psychological tendencies can overwhelm sound judgment. Narcissists, for example, have an inflated estimate of their own abilities. They are forced to limp through life accommodating the gap between what they imagine they can do and what they actually can do. Depressed people, on the other hand, have a deflated estimate of their ability and suffer a corresponding gap between imagination and reality. To them, the world seems more imposing and severe than it really is. Most people fall somewhere between these two psychological limits.

Whatever your psychological state, Chapter 9 emphasizes that you never really *know* without actually acting. A critical part of the emotional course is learning how to modify the experiment to account for unexpected influences, how to draw proper conclusions, and how to determine when the experiment is "working."

Further, Chapter 9 insists that *you* are conducting the experiment. It cannot be delegated to someone else without paying severe penalties. Only *you* can say what your goals and values are. Only *you* can say to what degree you are willing to exert yourself or sacrifice other things to achieve a goal.

Chapter 10 is an *emotional training course* for dealing with setbacks, crises, and failure. You'll learn how to handle the negative factors that accompany any worthwhile course of action. For crisis situations, this chapter gives practical rules of thumb that can save you from foolish or costly actions in moments of vulnerability.

Most important, you'll learn how to redefine failure, how to qualify it so as to allow yourself to risk again, how to profit from it, how to consider it as vital information, and how not to consider it as a judgment on your ability or worth.

By interpreting failure properly, you'll know when to:

■ Accept certain losses and move on

■ Try harder

■ Redefine the experiment ("try differently")

■ Abandon a lost cause

In Chapter 11, you'll learn the importance of affirming your decisions. Affirmations help you express the validity of your goals in a world that is largely indifferent to them. Affirmations help you feel comfortable in stating, pursuing, and satisfying your needs. Chapter 11 helps you make affirmations that work for *you* in particular, that enhance your morale in *your* particular situation.

Chapter 12 explains that decisions *integrate* who we are on the inside with what our actions are on the outside. Thus, every time we make decisions wisely, we affirm our true nature and gain the confidence to take larger and more substantial steps. We become more skilled at visualizing a goal—and then bringing it into our own lives and into the lives of those close to us. The cycle of visualize-decide-actualize is a never-ending process that allows us to live without fear and hesitation.

The appendix contains a checklist for evaluating the quality of your decisions. By asking yourself the questions listed there, you'll be able to determine the adequacy of your approach and figure out which aspects of your decision making need further attention.

Taken together, the twelve methods presented in this book present a unique view of decision making. They show how to combine the wisdom of your rational mind and the strength of your emotions to develop decisions that are sound and more fulfilling. These methods will not make your problems go away, but they will make you much more capable of handling your problems on an everyday basis.

Before we start, I would like to emphasize an important point. What I hope you carry away from these pages is an *attitude toward decision making* rather than a rigid set of rules. Although the methods presented here have helped many people in many situations, you and your situation may differ in essential ways. Accordingly, I encourage you to consider these methods as starting points in your own life. Be open to those methods that speak directly to your situation. Experiment with them and see how you can make them work for you. I will consider my effort in writing this book rewarded if you can gain just one pivotal idea— one that makes a difference—from reading it.

ACKNOWLEDGMENTS

I wish to acknowledge those who have helped me in my career and given me the encouragement to explore new ideas and areas.

I am grateful to the University of Massachusetts Staff Training and Development Group for encouraging me to give a series of seminars on effective decision making in 1989 and 1990.

I am also thankful to my partner, Kathleen Wheaton, for moral support in completing this book.

I am indebted to Barbara Dailey, Jack Dixon, Sid Kaye, Len Kaye, Charles Kaye, Len Schwab, Mary Sunderland, John Willig, and Kathleen Wheaton for reading the manuscript of this book and offering helpful comments and suggestions. Particular thanks is due to Len Schwab and my brother, Sid Kaye, who reviewed the manuscript in detail and contributed many refinements and clarifications.

H.K.

1

RECOGNIZE CONFUSION AND ANXIETY

CONFUSION CONTAINS A USEFUL MESSAGE

When you are confused, it feels like your compass is spinning. Events challenge your present course of action so thoroughly that your vision becomes fogged. You can't see things clearly. You're unsure of the *meaning* of these happenings and how you should respond. The ground seems to be shifting underneath your feet. Much of your emotional energy becomes absorbed in an effort merely to hold on, to steady yourself.

Thinking about the situation and discussing it with others doesn't seem to help. Even if an impending crisis is perceived and acknowledged by everyone, there is rarely any agreement about your best response. The question, "What should I do?" rolls around and around in your head, but all options appear vague and untenable.

Emotional programs overrun rational thought completely at this point, leaving you feeling vulnerable. You may even get angry with yourself for not being able to formulate the issues in a way that leads to a decision. Or you may become impatient, feeling that there must be a quick-fix or magic solution that will effortlessly extract you from the negative situation. It seems tempting to revert to a familiar childhood trick: Find someone to save you, to take responsibility for your choices.

If this sounds depressing, don't worry, for this is good news: Knowing that you're confused is very important information. Be thankful for your confusion! Before you were able to recognize your confusion, you might have been able to repress the knowledge that certain things in your life were not working, that certain lights on your master control panel were flashing emergency red. Confusion is a blessing in disguise because it's a second chance at capturing your attention. Confusion asks, "Are you sure you've got this right, kiddo?"

Confusion is *unconscious* knowledge that you need to act on a situation. If this knowledge were conscious, you would be obliged to accept the challenge, along with the many risks accompanying it. Confusion invites your conscious mind to examine the methods by which you have previously avoided acting on the problem. ("Oh, it's okay to operate the machine with that red light flashing—it's just how the machine *is*.")

Often the confusion is due to a sudden loss. No matter whether the loss involves your job, romantic relationship, lifetime savings, loved ones, physical health, or your house burning down, the result is disorientation. You are stunned. The reality upon which you depended is suddenly changed. How are you to make such a major adjustment to a new reality?

Other events that often precipitate confusion are failure, disappointment, and rejection. Each event requires you to re-evaluate previous decisions, since the assumptions on which they were based may now be different. The event alters your situation and indicates that your present course is no longer acceptable. You must change.

The unacceptability of your present course means you're unsatisfied with the ways your needs and goals are being met. Or perhaps you're in a situation that threatens your well-being or survival. In either case, we shall shortly see how the decision-making process translates these unmet needs into goals.

Confusion arises when it appears that there is no easy way to address these new goals. Feeling confused is truly annoying: Many options occur as possibilities, but none appears to be a reasonably good choice. Further, it's not certain that any of the options will satisfy the newly defined needs. Indeed, the hidden drawbacks of these options may cause more discomfort than your current situation.

Confusion is a blessing in disguise: It's a second chance at capturing your attention on a very important problem.

The first step in addressing confusion is recognizing that you're spinning your wheels, seeing that you're going round and round the same emotional loop. The second step is to gain perspective on the problem. Sometimes this can be gained by talking the problem over with a stranger, a person who has no preconceptions about you or the situation. Another way to gain perspective is simply to refrain from responding in the customary manner. If the situation allows it, jump out of the loop and see what happens. The third step is to accept the challenge and see if you can formulate the problem in a way that can bring a solution. Chapter 2 gives many specific ways to accomplish this.

HOW DECISION ANXIETY ARISES

You're at a fork in the road, trying to decide whether to go down path A or B. Anxiety is the roadside bandit that keeps you stuck at the junction, unable to move forward. Anxiety arises because both paths have negative features that can be avoided only by staying put. Neither option is totally acceptable. As psychologist Rollo May observes in *The Meaning of Anxiety* (see Suggested Reading List), "The essence of the 'trapped' feeling in . . . anxiety is that the individual is threatened whichever way he turns" (p. 315).

When you're in the grasp of anxiety, you feel like a yo-yo. First you decide on path A, and an hour later you decide on path B. This switching back and forth happens so fast that no real progress is ever made. There's an uncanny sense of *déjà vu*. You're thinking the same thoughts, feeling the same emotions, as yesterday—but nothing changes.

The anxious person *hesitates*. He or she is held immobile by the nonact of "deciding." Deliberation is far safer than propelling oneself into action. Yet, the nonaction of anxiety is not relaxing. Anxiety will not allow you to sit by the side of the road and enjoy the flowers. Anxiety is debilitating because it holds you immobile and, at the same time, pressures you to move. It insists, "Hurry up! Make up your mind, or a catastrophe will overcome you."

Anxiety may be a problem for you if you are:

1. Easily distracted from important tasks

2. Obsessive about smoking, drinking, eating, sex, shopping, TV, or work

3. Unable to make any plans at all

4. Irritable

5. Constantly looking for magic shortcuts

6. Regularly overburdening your friends with your problems

7. Always feeling like you *must* do something right away

8. Forever unable to do what you say you're going to do

9. Overwhelmed by problems that seem hopelessly complex

10. Experiencing headaches, ulcers, or insomnia

Anxiety is a part of everyday life. It's manifested in personal health, work, romance, family relations, finances, environmental concerns, and government. Although everyone experiences anxiety to varying degrees, it's "neurotic" only when one is crippled by it. This book is primarily concerned with anxiety as it affects the decision-making process of reasonably well-adjusted individuals, not as a neurotic phenomenon. (For the more general implications of anxiety and its clinical treatment, see Rollo May's previously mentioned classic study.)

Anxiety is generated when you perceive that you're in a situation in which your choices are severely constricted—or in which you have no apparent choices—and in which the possibility of suffering looms high. Thus, anxiety deals with the situation of *helplessness*. The emotional connotations of helplessness are extremely significant in determining our reactions to anxiety.

As adults, we experience anxiety in many varying contexts, but its underlying emotional significance is unchanging: Anxieties always refer back to childhood survival issues. Although your present situation may be totally different from these early contexts, they're still capable of seizing control of your emotional apparatus. As infants, we first experience anxiety when we are faced with dangers we can neither comprehend nor resist. The resulting sense of being helpless and vulnerable creates a profound rift in our consciousness. Just as we become aware of ourselves as individuals ("I can"), we also become aware of our mental and physical limitations ("I can't"). As infants, we depend on others to save us.

The emotional environment provided by parents contributes greatly to the infant's reactions to anxiety. Ideally, parents provide sufficient soothing and attention to allow their infant to leap successfully the many small hurdles of dealing with anxiety. Because the environment varies so strongly from family to family—and even from sibling to sibling within the same family—each person's anxiety cues and threshold are different. Some people become anxious at the slightest provocation. Even the smallest incident of helplessness or least hint of threat causes them misery. They hate having to compromise even on minor issues. Other people can tolerate far worse with ease. They're able to soothe themselves in moments of uncertainty and helplessness and are more resistant to the stress of imminent danger.

There are relatively few parental behaviors that foster anxiety in the infant. As noted developmental psychologist Donald Winnicott explains, most mothers are "good enough." By adulthood, though, an underlying anxiety can become manifest in many different ways, some of which are very subtle. For example, a child who is forced to do many things against its will tends to develop, as an adult, a compensating anxiety that equates committing to relationships with loss of self. In their psyche, the nickel of pleasure gained from the relationship is outweighed by the dime of anticipated pain. Although they *want* closeness, they withdraw from it instead. It's easier than running the risk of being crushed by the relationship. They save themselves from the kinds of losses they suffered as a child, but at the cost of never being able to claim any gain. Their stated goal of being in a relationship is undermined by an even greater, yet unconscious, goal: avoiding pain. They "win" by simply not playing the game.

Being able to describe the origin of your anxiety and the way it manifests in your life will usually not make it disappear. You can describe this *dis*-ease with clinical precision and philosophical insight, but to overcome it, you have to gain the courage to risk acting in spite of it. One goal of this book is to help you face anxiety, gain the useful message it has for you, and move on to tackling the risks that it has prevented you from acknowledging.

These are not easy tasks. In my own case, anxiety has proven to be a vexing companion. My anxiety issue centers around an aversion to self-promotion, even when it's necessary and appropriate. Over the years, I've observed that when it comes time to do promotion, I distract myself with a never-ending task: I spend all my time "preparing," trying to become smart enough. In this way, I avoid facing a basic sociological truth: Without some promotion, the well-being of any person, company, or group is diminished. Promotion is not vain egotism, but a valid effort to gain the attention of an intended audience. It allows you to bring yourself, your products, or your group to the marketplace.

For years, I operated on an anxiety-provoking and false premise: "If I'm really good enough, people will discover it by themselves. They will come to me without my having to make a claim." This way, I never exposed myself to the risk of being rejected. The only problem was that the world doesn't operate this way!

A high-anxiety maneuver: Deny yourself the satisfaction of your needs and goals by saying that

- You don't deserve them.
- You don't have enough ability to achieve them.
- Your present obligations to others prevent you from taking any risks.
- The problem is not bad enough to warrant attention.

On the outside, these denials keep the boat from rocking, but on the inside, anxiety can reach the boiling point: You're suffering and not allowing yourself to do anything about it!

Anxiety will not subside to manageable levels until you start to *act on the real issues*. Simply making plans won't help. Likewise, taking indiscriminate action won't help. Actions that don't directly address the real issues only maintain the anxiety. They serve as a smoke screen for avoiding the risks.

The final measure of whether an action is appropriate to reducing anxiety is gained only by doing it and then observing its effect. This measure has little relation to whether your overall plans are being fulfilled. It depends more on the way you respond psychologically to multiple objectives and demands on your attention.

On the psychological level, anxieties always refer back to *survival* issues.

SORTING OUT THE MESSAGES

Your situation may change, but seeing that a problem exists is a matter of vision. You must *recognize* that there is a problem!

Three young women were attending a college lecture on problem solving. The professor posed a test of their reasoning ability.

"Suppose that you're aboard a small boat alone in the Pacific Ocean. You spot a ship approaching with several thousand sex-starved sailors on board. What would you do to avoid any problems?"

"I would turn my craft in the opposite direction," said the redhead.

"I would pass them, but display my knife to show my intention to protect myself," said the brunette.

"Frankly," murmured the blonde, "I understand the situation, but I fail to see the problem."

How do you sort out the messages contained in confusion? The messages are telling you that something is wrong or needs to be modified. But what *is* that something? The answer lies in being able to access your needs and feelings.

Your feelings and needs are the key to *identifying* more precisely what the problem is. This is not as easy as it sounds. Past emotional habits can make it difficult to access your feelings. After years of looking at things in a habitual way, they lose perspective: Obstacles that can be overcome with reasonable effort may appear completely insurmountable. You may see yourself as a victim of circumstances, unable to take effective action. You may see only your liabilities and constraints, instead of your assets and resources. Or you may not see yourself as worthy of attaining the very goals that could make you happy.

When you are confused, your emotions and fears work against your intelligence. Sorting out the issues takes a certain amount of concentration. (Note: At this stage, you haven't even formulated the problem. You're only saying what the problem is *about*.) In the midst of confusion, it's all too easy to focus on the obstacles. Without attention, your intelligence does not have a chance to gather up the required bits of evidence and piece them together.

Sorting out the messages means distinguishing the meaningful pattern from the surrounding distractions. It is an act of discrimination. It is a limiting of your field of vision and experience. You filter out the irrelevant. Emotional awareness is needed to make these distinctions. You need to ask yourself:

- What is not as it should be?
- Why is it unsatisfactory to me?
- What needs of mine are not being met?
- Is it within my power to do anything about it?

Confusion is often accompanied by excess emotional stress. When we're overstressed, we lose the ability to pay close attention. We become easily distracted. Annoyances and minor chores scatter our attention and prevent us from concentrating. We miss the message by becoming vulnerable to small insults to our vanity and by failing to recognize when significant needs are not being met. Sorting out the messages gets at the underlying problem by affirming your right to satisfy these unmet needs.

Sorting out the messages is the key to understanding the "two-voices dilemma." One voice says "Do it! Risk a change." The other voice says, "No way, stay in your place!" Which voice do you listen to? Which represents your best interests?

Even accomplished decision makers hear these two voices in decisions that involve significant risk to self-esteem. Taken individually, each voice is articulate and persuasive. Both cannot be followed simultaneously, yet it's rarely clear which voice should be heeded.

The trick is to look at the message each voice represents and examine its relevance to the decision at hand. In general, *changing* is the choice that involves greater growth and, also, greater risk. *Staying in place*, on the other hand, also has merit. Perhaps your dissatisfaction stems from unrealistic expectations. If you're satisfying your basic needs within the situation, accommodating or enduring its negative aspects may be sensible options. In all cases, emotional awareness of your situation and of how well your needs are being met is the foundation for interpreting the voices and identifying the true nature of the problem.

ACCEPTING THE CHALLENGE TO GROW

A major concept in decision making is that of personal responsibility. Some aspects of your life are within your power to change; others are not. The differences are usually not spelled out for you. Most often, you must decide for yourself.

We tend to forget that, in many respects, we *choose* what happens in our own lives. Especially in long-term relationships involving job and family, we lose consciousness of our ability to take initiative. We become habituated to reacting instead of acting. When negative situations occur, we try to adjust as well as we can, ignore the problem, or back-pedal. If a further problem arises, we feel trapped. In our efforts to be accommodating, we have reached our limit. The habitual response must be abandoned and a new one exercised. Feelings of helplessness are accompanied by anger and frustration: How could things have gotten to this point? Is this the straw that breaks the camel's back? Is now the time to take firmer initiative? You know you must do something. It feels scary, though, to act without fully understanding the situation and without guaranteed results.

We assign our confusion to the new event. In reality, it is the entire series of steps (decisions) made up to that point that has created the dilemma. *We* are responsible, not the external event. When you can see this, you begin to make progress in becoming an active agent in your own decision making. You have accepted the challenge of change.

Excessive activity is one means by which accepting the challenge is often avoided. In *Management and the Activity Trap* (1974), management expert George Odiorne describes how American business has become stifled by activity for its own sake. Goals become lost in the swirl of activity. Because the activity is often mere busy work, the company's well-being is not advanced. This phenomenon is not limited to business. Professionals in all fields stand the risk of becoming enmeshed in narrow niches where they lose perception of their general goals. As specialists, they master a limited range of activities and feel comfortable within it. But they cannot change when the market (or their personal values) calls for a new activity.

The activity trap shows itself in personal choices too. Whenever we allow ourselves to be fooled by substituting motion for progress, busyness for purposeful activity, we fall into it. Most people on the outside are fooled, so we try to fool ourselves. On the inside, we are starving for a way to bring our activity more in line with our inner purpose. We want to be able to accept the challenges that can provide genuine satisfaction.

GAINING CLARITY

A strange thing: When you accept a challenge in the proper way, confusion disappears. When clarity is gained, the various and sundry influences acting on you become resolved. You can see the things that you must work to change and the things that you must accept as they are. The road ahead does not necessarily become easy, but at least it becomes clearly visible.

THE TWO-VOICES DILEMMA

STAY IN PLACE

- Wait for the right moment
- It's the safe thing to do

- Hope for a miracle to get me out of this mess
- Think about it some more

- Keep my options open

Benefits

1. Keep the peace

2. Maintain face

3. Avoid criticism
4. Harder to fail this way

5. Eliminate stress of openly claiming my values

Liabilities

1. Develop ulcers

2. Never get a chance to succeed
3. Lose self-esteem

4. Forced to accept ever greater losses to maintain current position

RISK A CHANGE

- Exercise more initiative
- Act on my own best judgment
- Accept the challenge of change
- Learn if the change will provide the results I want

Benefits

1. Gain the chance to succeed
2. Gain self-esteem from being the agent of power in my own life

3. Eliminate negatives
4. Become capable at change

Liabilities

1. I can fall on my face. Then everyone will cry, "Shame."
2. I'll have to compromise my other goals.
3. The change may not bring the desired satisfaction. I could discover I was deceiving myself.

When you gain clarity, it feels as if you have suddenly become powerful. This feeling reflects the true situation. For, *with clarity, you are no longer wasting effort* by

- Trying to change things that can't be changed
- *Not* acting on things that should and can be changed

Clarity is gained through attention and knowledge, but the big question is: Attention to what? Knowledge of what? It is said that sages have powers of attention so great that they can directly perceive the truth about any situation. Their attention to detail and concentration allow them to see that which is not completely manifest. This may be possible for a Buddha, but the rest of us are constrained by our limitations. For us, choice is stressful, because we must act in the midst of our confusion and in spite of our uncertainty. Waiting until we are enlightened or have full knowledge is not realistic!

Attention to the pros and cons of a situation is not enough to ensure clarity. You may possess the attention to detail and concentration of a Sherlock Holmes, but to gain clarity, you must be able to pay attention to your needs and goals and how well you are meeting them.

Neither is knowledge of facts ("objective truth") sufficient to gain clarity. Even if you could memorize the entire encyclopedia or solve complicated calculus problems in your head, you would not necessarily attain clarity.

Clarity is not the same as logical certainty. If you are absolutely certain of the consequences of a choice, there is really no choice and no stress; you will pursue the most advantageous option. Moreover, clarity is not achieved by trying to determine your ability to achieve a goal in advance of any motion. Prolonged conjecture about your ability to achieve a goal is futile. You'll never know until you act with the full weight of your being.

To gain clarity, you need *self-knowledge*. That is, you need to know how to learn from your own experience. Some self-knowledge is gained by reflection, some by gaining a sense of your own capability through action. The knowledge that gives clarity is the knowledge that you can handle new situations and learn what you need as you go along.

Clarity results from *emotionally* resolving the conflicts contained within the decision process. It has little to do with logically figuring out the most useful course of action or with actual motion down that path. It comes instead when you've truly accepted the trade-offs implicit in pursuing that path. Acceptance means that you see the necessity of taking the whole package instead of picking and choosing parts of it.

> ## Clarity results from *emotionally* resolving the conflicts contained within the decision process.

Acceptance allows you to look at the negatives realistically rather than through the eyes of fear. With this realistic vision, you'll eventually find ways to minimize their effect and compensate for them. When you look at the negatives through the eyes of fear, they become unyielding and monolithic giants. You can't see any detailed structure that would allow a foothold on them so you can start to unravel them.

Another aspect of gaining clarity in decisions is your attitude toward the risks involved in pursuing an option. Talent and ability are not as important to eventual success as the willingness to accept a certain level of risk and possible failure. Becoming unstuck in decisions is often a matter of seeing that risk can't be totally eliminated by clever manipulation or elaborate strategies.

Once you commit to a path, opportunities you never even considered may come along and make your goal easier to achieve. Moreover, problems you never anticipated may arise, requiring sacrifices that make your goal harder to achieve. The ballast that steadies the boat throughout all this is *desire*. Desire provides the incentive to learn from your mistakes and modify your efforts so as to reach the destination.

Deciding has a strong component of desire. In the context of decisions, you *are* your desires. Either they materialize and fulfill you—or they fail to materialize and frustrate you.

It's easy to fall into the trap of telling yourself, "I don't have the resources needed to pursue this alternative. Therefore I will not try." Of course, without resources, failure is certain in most ventures. Yet, the best course of action may not be to give up, but to develop the resources systematically. Clarity allows you to see that sometimes preparation is necessary, that you must spend the time and effort to gather the necessary resources. Clarity allows you to apply patience and energy to your choices, even if other choices (of lesser interest) pay benefits more quickly. Clarity fosters good decisions by encouraging you to overcome the path of least resistance with insight and dedication.

In summary, this chapter has shown you how to overcome confusion by interpreting it as a message, "Something needs to be changed." It has shown you ways to bring decision anxiety down to manageable levels by acting on the real issues. And finally, it has introduced the notion of personal responsibility in decision making. You can gain clarity and conquer feelings of helplessness by accepting the challenge posed by the decision.

2

DEFINE THE DECISION
SO THAT IT ADDRESSES
THE REAL ISSUES

PLACE THE DECISION IN CONTEXT

Accepting the challenge of decision making means recognizing that you have a problem of sorts. In this chapter, you'll see why it's important to then *define* the problem so that it addresses the real issues.

Defining the problem involves both emotional and rational facets. The process recommended here is first to access the emotional facet, and then to develop a statement of the problem from it in rational terms. There is good reason for this two-step sequence. The problem means that you, as a person, feel some need is unfulfilled. Only you can truly gauge your own emotional reactions (in the form of hunger, need for safety, desires, fears, etc.). Although feelings are paramount in determining your needs and goals, they're not very powerful in helping you achieve them. To do that, you need to be able to *think* about the problem. Once a problem is stated in rational terms, it becomes more amenable to solution.

Placing the decision in context helps you determine the nature and extent of the problem. Like a good journalist, you want to know the basic facts that describe the situation:

- **What**: What happened? Which aspect of your life is concerned? (Health, employment, family, friends, spirit, finances, education, or other?) What are your reactions to this problem?

- **Where**: Does the problem occur in a specific place?

- **Who**: Does the problem concern only you? Does it concern your family, friends, coworkers, country? Does it concern your adversaries? Must you accept the problem as yours, or can you delegate it to others?

- **When**: Does the problem occur at particular times? Is it a problem that you anticipate will happen in the future? Does the problem deal with the past? How long will it last? Does it require immediate action?

- **Why**: Why is this a problem? Why did it happen? (Which conditions promoted its occurrence?) Why does it involve you?

Contexts are harder to define when they don't fall neatly into the usual ready-made categories. For example, on a feeling level, your problem may concern your spouse being angry with you for not earning enough money. It may not be obvious whether the real issue is your salary at work or your marital relationship (or both!). Yet, placing the decision in context may allow you to perceive a definite trend. On the one hand, your spouse may be angry with you over many other issues too. In such circumstances, it's likely that the underlying problem does not concern your salary. On the other hand, if your salary is the only issue that elicits anger from your partner, and you yourself feel bad about your salary in other respects, then salary may indeed be the issue. Because cause and effect are so closely intertwined in practice, it takes several penetrating questions to discriminate between categories, to get at the real issues.

Very often, you'll need to get more *information* in order to define the problem. The situation is like that of a doctor who listens to the patient's account of symptoms. The patient's informal description (and even a cursory physical exam) may not provide sufficient facts to allow the doctor to deduce the illness. The doctor may have to ask further questions and order further tests to make a diagnosis.

Don't think that gathering information is always easy and straightforward. It's no accident that the act of gathering information about military and industrial competitors is called *intelligence*. It requires a great deal of effort to find the information you need, to sort it out from the information you *don't* need, and to develop the means to distinguish the former from the latter.

As Richard Saul Wurman points out in his book *Information Anxiety* (see Suggested Reading List) there is an overabundance of information in our society. Powerful media merchants play on our fear of being found ignorant and pressure us to buy even more information. As a society, we're obsessed with being informed and keeping up with the latest advances, because we're afraid of appearing deficient in our knowledge.

The psychological issue underlying information anxiety is that of power. In times past, the person who knew more was more powerful. In present times, the person who knows more is simply a person who has filled his or her head with more information. The person may know ten times more information than is needed to navigate through life. At parties, the *infomaniac* can impress others with juicy tidbits of information and feel adequately "literate." In other areas of life, the very same person may have great difficulty sorting out all those facts to use them gainfully.

Information *is* important because it announces changes that may affect us. Yet, with so much information available in our society, why isn't it the magic key to better decision making? The answer is that information has *value* that depends on the situation. It's up to us to determine how relevant the information is and what its meaning is.

Meaning uncovers patterns, trends, relationships—and allows us to predict the influence of important events. Meaning defines how the information relates to us and our future actions. We use meanings to justify our actions, to assign value judgments to factual happenings, and to choose one course of action over another.

There is a point of diminishing return with the task of gathering information. A certain amount of knowledge is essential for effective decisions. Beyond that, gaining more knowledge actually works against you. It sidetracks you from the task at hand and hampers the boldness and self-confidence needed to address unknown obstacles as they arise. We all want guarantees in the face of uncertainty. What carries us through is not complete and certain knowledge, but faith in our projects and trust that we will be able to work out the problems we encounter.

Information gathering can be misused as a form of procrastination. It's possible to research the problem to death:

> The philosopher Immanuel Kant (1724–1804) was still a bachelor at the age of fifty. A neighbor offered the hand in marriage of his beautiful daughter to the scholar, who had already achieved fame throughout Germany for his masterpiece, *The Critique of Pure Reason*. Kant replied, "What a splendid offer. Let me consider its merits, and I will get back to you when I've made my decision."

> Kant studied the state of marriage, its virtues, its moral significance, and its financial liabilities. He researched the joys of offspring and marriage's place in the human drama. *Five years* later, he finished his deliberations. He was ready. The only problem was that, in the meantime, the neighbor's daughter had found a sweetheart, married, and given birth to two children.

The concept of *proportional response* helps you figure out how much information you should gather: The time and effort spent should be roughly proportional to the decision's significance in your life. For example, deciding what to eat at a restaurant should take no more than a few minutes. Perhaps the only research you may do is to ask the waiter about the specials of the day or about the available salad dressings. On the other hand, if you're deciding on a midlife career change, you'll need much more information. You'll need an understanding of the costs, efforts, liabilities, and payoffs, as well as the resources and opportunities available to you. Because this decision could conceivably impact the rest of your life, the information-gathering phase should take months instead of minutes. The research effort would then be proportional to the importance of that project in your life.

ORGANIZE THE IMPORTANT INFORMATION

Man does not live by data alone. The motive behind assembling the basic facts (where, when, what, who, why) is to *organize* the information in a useful way. When information is organized, it allows you to better understand:

- What's happening right now? (diagnosis)
- Why or how did this happen? (etiology)
- What options are available to us? (prescription)
- What is the likely result for each option? (prognosis)

The words in parentheses indicate the medical terminology for the decision-making process. They emphasize that decision making deals with definite mental processes that allow us to appraise situations, consider the options, and make recommendations for the best course of action.

Organizing your information is particularly important when you're dealing with complex decisions. By structuring the data into categories, you'll be able to use it to develop correlations and cause-effect relationships. With the information arranged this way, you're less likely to be overwhelmed by the huge mass of information that accompanies complex decisions. Your courses of action will become more apparent. Additionally, you can see if the parts are consistent and predictable, or contradictory and haphazard. Such observations can lead to the need for additional information or to tests to resolve the differences.

Once you've assembled the raw data, you can apply logic and insight to refine it. This "data processing" step considers the following factors:

- **Relevance**: Does the information address the significant issues? Does it consider your perspective or situation?
- **Accuracy**: Is the source credible? Can the information be verified?
- **Completeness**: Does it cover the entire scope that you are considering?

- **Discernment**: Does it show the differences between or among the options?
- **Timeliness**: Is the information dated or obsolete?
- **Representativeness**: Are a few pieces of information sufficient to predict the rest? If so, you can save effort by sampling rather than completing an exhaustive survey.

Be it in business, medicine, warfare, or romance, accurate appraisal of the situation is often the key to resolving a decision dilemma. In fact, once a situation is correctly diagnosed, the problem can usually be resolved by following any number of standard techniques.

Appraising the situation correctly, however, is not simple! You will need *intelligence* to understand the difference between your situation and that of other people in similar situations. You will need *experience* to know the many possible ways the facts can be interpreted. You will need to exert *effort* to dig out the necessary information or to do experiments that will reveal it to you. Finally, you will need *courage* to see things as they are, in contrast to seeing things as you wish they might be. (If all this seems overwhelming to you, don't despair! You will improve with practice, and help can be obtained from friends, family, coworkers, and professional counselors, who can act as sounding boards for your own interpretations.)

FORMULATE THE DECISION AS A PROBLEM

The first dictionary definition of the word *problem* is, "any matter involving uncertainty, doubt, or difficulty." It reflects the most common usage, which considers a problem merely as a troublesome situation. The second dictionary definition is, "a question proposed for solution or discussion." Although less common, this definition is better suited to the decision-making process. Without denying the difficulty, it says that a problem is something more:

A problem is a question in search of an answer.

A two-year-old infant may have a problem, but often, at that age, the infant cannot express *what* the problem is. This doesn't mean that the problem doesn't exist. The ability to verbalize the problem, to pose the question, requires intellectual capacity that the infant does not yet possess.

Adults, who have the ability to handle concepts, can pinpoint the problem so that it can be better addressed. If you refuse to apply your intellect to your problems, you'll be like that two-year-old who can only point to its tummy and say "hurts."

Many people revert to this childhood mode, in effect, when they pose their problem in terms of the conflicting options. Consider, for example, the following decision statement: "I would like to accept this wonderful job offer, but it means moving to a different state. If I accept, my family will be very upset over the relocation. If I do not accept, I'll be upset over losing a rare opportunity."

This is not really a definition of the problem, but a description of the conflict between two options that have already been selected. It's very easy to fall into this trap, because the conflicting aspects of the obvious alternatives are always more visible and concrete than the goals.

Defining the problem in terms of the conflict is dangerous because you are struggling with the options before you have stated what you're trying to accomplish. If you struggle with the conflict, there is a good chance that *both* choices may be unsatisfactory.

The problem must be defined in terms of needs, not conflicting situations. In the example, the underlying need is for meaningful employment. Once the problem has been defined in this way, *all* the options can be measured against how well that need is addressed. The conflicts themselves are only obstacles to be overcome or accepted.

Stating the problem in terms of your needs transforms it into a goal statement that can be handled by the power of your rational mind to great advantage. But don't lose sight of the fact that your intellect will be of little use in *accessing* what your needs are. For that, you must rely on your emotional apparatus: your feelings, your sense of yourself, and your reactions to the world around you. Advanced logic won't help you know you are hungry. All that is required is being in touch with your own bodily signals.

Because effective decision making is part rational and part feeling, there are *two* ways it can become unbalanced. In the first, the person trusts and uses his or her feelings much more than intellect. In the second, the situation is reversed. The person relies on his or her rational thought process, but can't access emotions.

There's a point at which gaining more knowledge works against effective decision making.

Very few people achieve a good balance between thought and emotion. Intellectuals are notoriously poor decision makers. They usually skip the phase of decision making that deals with needs and feelings because they have become accustomed to the use of rational doubt. Mistrust of their emotions inhibits their ability to decide. They see too many subtleties, too many uncertainties, too many unknowns that must be researched before action can be taken. Extensive knowledge of what can go wrong works against taking simple action. As a result, underlying needs are converted into intellectual problems ("pseudoneeds") that are often totally irrelevant. Although intellectuals are adept at manipulating complex problems and applying convoluted logic, the problem they define may not address the real issues!

Feeling-oriented people, on the other hand, often mistrust their own intelligence. They base their decisions on what they feel like doing at the moment, on what others do, and on what others advise them to do.

Do not confuse alternatives with the statement of the problem. If you do, the resulting set of alternatives will be greatly impoverished. For example, suppose you're in a room that is at 40 degrees Fahrenheit and you are wearing only light clothing. You feel cold and uncomfortable. The problem is: "This room is too cold for me." Some possible alternatives are:

- Put on heavier clothes
- Adjust the thermostat
- Build a fire in the fireplace
- Leave the room for one that is warmer
- Tolerate this condition (if you'll be there only a few minutes)

If you tell yourself that the problem is that you must put on, find, or buy heavier clothes, you have effectively eliminated the other options. By seizing one alternative as the "problem," you may overlook other solutions that are simpler or more effective.

There are many people who can say—with great accuracy—how someone else should solve a problem, but who are unable to solve it in their own case. Thomas J. D'Zurilla, in his book, *Problem Solving Therapy*,[1] notes that problem-solving *performance* is not necessarily equal to problem-solving *ability*.

Problem solving is an important *part* of decision making, but it's not the whole story. Decision making contains the added dimension of imputing the self into the situation. Those who are weak in will or who lack sufficient self-integration to stand behind their decisions, often hope that an impersonal problem-solving method (perhaps even a problem-solving computer!) will solve their problem *for* them.

While it's true that other people and computers can "make your decision for you," it's unlikely that the resulting decision will reflect the subjective aspects that you bring to the particular situation.

STRUCTURE THE PROBLEM TO CUT IT DOWN TO SIZE

Kathleen walked into the room, looking like the end of the world had arrived. She cried, "The deal is off. My lawyer just called and said that the person who contracted to buy my house has decided to back down. I'm devastated. I've already made plans and commitments that depend on the deal going through on schedule. I don't know what to do."

"Well," I said, "People don't just suddenly decide to back out of a deal, especially after they've placed a nonrefundable

---

[1] New York: Springer Publishing Co., 1986.

deposit of $15,000. Let's find out what the facts are. Ask your lawyer to call the buyer and inquire about the details of her situation."

The next day, the lawyer told Kathleen, "It's a problem with financing. The buyer can't sell her own house as quickly as she would like, and she doesn't have quite enough cash to complete the deal. She is sixty-five years old. She was recently widowed and would like to buy your house because it is closer to her children."

Now the problem had more *structure*. It wasn't that the buyer didn't want the house. It was a matter of money and timing. I told Kathleen, "Call your lawyer and ask him to phone the buyer again. See if he can find out how much money is needed. (We knew that the buyer intended to buy the house outright with no mortgage.) Would she consider applying to a local bank for a mortgage to cover her temporarily? Could she borrow that amount from her children? Or could she take out an equity loan on her present house?"

A week later, the lawyer called back. He said, "Good news! The buyer never considered getting a mortgage. She assumed that a mortgage was out of the question, considering her age and the fact that she didn't have a job. She didn't know that banks will give a mortgage to anyone whose equity position is strong enough, regardless of age or job status. So, she applied for a mortgage at a local bank and received it without difficulty. The deal is *on*."

Once you have sketched the context of your decision and formulated it as a problem, you can structure it to cut it down to size. Structuring uses the principle of "divide and conquer." By breaking the decision up into smaller parts and becoming familiar with how each part works, you can cut a large and intractable decision down to size.

By examining the details, you will be able to see parts of the decision that can be implemented immediately, parts that must be further researched, parts that require wait-and-see actions, and parts that require a prerequisite series of actions. Further, you may become aware that certain parts simply can't be changed under the present circumstances, no matter how hard you try. Efforts in these parts should naturally be suspended until your situation changes.

Here are the basic questions used in structuring problems:

1. What factors are needed to state the problem?

2. How does each factor affect the decision outcome?

3. How much control do you have over each factor?

4. What else determines the condition of each factor?

5. What impact do your personal values have on the way you evaluate each factor?

6. What conditions determine the outcome?

Structuring provides texture, character, connection, and relevance to the problem. Once you have structured a problem, it's easier to understand how each part works. You can place it in a different perspective. Like making a three-dimensional model, you can walk around it, look at it from different angles, and see which sides present the most reward or least resistance. By approaching the problem on the most favorable side, you take advantage of its natural features and spare yourself the effort of scaling it at its steepest point.

Notice that, at this point, you have not tried to solve the problem. You have only stated it as accurately and completely as you can. Once a problem has been stated in a well-posed manner, the options for solutions come forth much more naturally.

After stating the decision context, the next stage of the thought process is *simplifying*. Focus attention on the major factors, the ones that most clearly determine the nature of the problem.

Reduce the amount of data by *identifying similarities*. The goal is to extract the useful data from a large set of experiences that are similar if not exactly the same. By lumping together experiences into broad categories, you reduce the amount of data to the point where it is handled more easily. You can select a representative case when the variability in the whole data set is small.

Try to establish cause-effect relations by decomposing the problem into parts. The key to this task is looking for and recognizing patterns: Does the problem occur under a certain set of conditions? Is this always so? (The exception can tell you as much as the rule!) By what mechanism is the effect produced? Which elements of the situation are coincidental?

Use logic to reduce the complexity of a problem. In everyday situations, we experience so many facets of a situation that we often lose the ability to draw obvious conclusions. Rarely will the evidence be so straightforward that we can directly perceive the bottom line. One way to overcome this is to use logic to draw inferences, even in fuzzy situations.

The art of inference is to extract the essential theme from the limited information that is available. It is like the doctor making a diagnosis and then a prognosis. If the doctor waits for absolute, 100 percent certainty before he makes a recommendation for medication or treatment, it may be too late. By the time every piece of information is available, the game may be over, the patient may already be dead. The doctor's challenge is to draw the inference so that action may be taken in a timely manner.

The decision you are making must be *specific*, or you'll find it impossible to sort out the issues and make concrete plans. For example, the decision "Whether or not to be a writer?" is poorly posed in this sense. There are too many unresolved issues! A better question would be, "Should I spend an hour each night for the next two weeks writing that sports article I've had on my mind?" This latter decision will not overwhelm your ability to respond and sets a concrete goal, a deadline, and a schedule to accomplish the goal.

Decisions that are too general are often attempts to "will" yourself out of a current reality by putting on a hat with a different label. In most situations, things don't work this way. "Deciding" to be a writer, baseball superstar, or corporation president is fine and good, but getting the world to go along with it may be substantially more difficult.

Don't expect a *single* decision to eliminate completely a long-standing or complex problem. By focusing on specific goals, one aims for "major improvement" rather than instant relief. Further goals can be set to improve and refine the mileage already gained.

WILL SOLUTION OF THE STATED PROBLEM BRING SATISFACTION?

At this stage, it's important to define what constitutes a solution to the problem. That is, you need to know what would be a satisfactory outcome. Criteria for this are discussed at length in Chapter 4. For the moment, I'd like to say that there is an important preliminary. It is making sure that you are working on the correct problem. If you successfully solve the wrong problem, you'll be no closer to satisfaction.

> A married man went to see a specialist in internal medicine. "Doctor," he exclaimed, "I'm really desperate! Last week, I came home from work and found my wife in bed with another man. When she saw me, she started weeping and begged me to forgive her. So I said, 'Well, let's have some coffee' . . ."
>
> "Then, the other night, the same thing! She was in bed with my neighbor! I took a pistol to kill them, but she cried and cried, so I said, 'Well, let's have some coffee' . . ."
>
> "Last night, I couldn't believe it! The same thing again! She promised me it was the last time. She said she'd never do it again, so I said, 'Well, let's have some coffee' . . ."
>
> "Doctor, I am very upset! Is it okay to drink this much coffee?"

In decision making, asking the *right* questions is essential. Irrelevant questions serve only as distractions. Without learning how to ask yourself the right questions, you may preoccupy yourself with issues that are totally peripheral to a successful solution. Sharp questions about the issues force you to discard injustice collecting, define your constraints, and set priorities in a way that will indicate clear action.

Many people who are deciding whether to leave an unrewarding job or marriage spend too much time collecting injustices. They reinforce what they already know ("I can't wait to get out of this bad situation") but refuse to examine concrete steps to action. They focus on escape from a negative situation instead of long-term strategies to achieve a positive one.

If you successfully solve the wrong problem, you will be no closer to satisfaction.

Wishful thinking affects the way we define decisions to ourselves. With wishful thinking, we have difficulty distinguishing between *wants* and *needs*. Wishful thinking allows us to fool ourselves about the real issues. Addressing our wants in many contexts is perfectly appropriate ("I want vanilla ice cream, not chocolate"). Yet, in larger decision contexts, the satisfaction of the wants may not lead to the desired results. Paying close attention to your needs improves your chances of making good decisions.

People often select the wrong problem out of wishful thinking. (See Chapter 9 for specific ways to avoid this trap.) *People engage in wishful thinking out of the desire for a magic solution.* That is, they choose an alternative because it's what they *want* to do, without considering whether it solves the problem (i.e., satisfies their real needs). Even if that alternative works in the sense of satisfying that want, they don't notice whether that alternative allows them to satisfy their needs. They will be forced to repress and deny certain feelings of unhappiness.

Here's where the "magic" comes in: They presume that satisfying *wants* will automatically satisfy *needs*. For many people, the *wants* deal with status (becoming a big-shot, a star, or a virtuoso performer) or safety issues (maintaining an invulnerable position). Both push people toward isolation. *Needs*, on the other hand, deal with reaching out to the environment. They require maintaining face-to-face relationships with others in which mutual benefits are exchanged.

The status performer will have none of this. He or she unconsciously hopes that the admiration of other people will provide the satisfaction that only real relationship can bring. Unfortunately, the admiration gained from being "special" is a very weak kind of relatedness. The talented prima ballerina, movie star, or world champion athlete is admired from afar, but usually remains inaccessible to closeness. True relationship involves vulnerability, risk, and commitment to others.

Those who are neurotically sensitive to failure also avoid facing their real needs. Instead, they rationalize the relatively conflict-free satisfaction of their *wants*. They fool themselves about their choices, because they tell themselves, "I'm doing what I want." They *choose,* but without regard for which choices provide real nourishment. Such choices are not truly free. The very options that could satisfy real needs are avoided.

Many pop psychology books insist that you can make all your dreams come true, that you can do anything you want.

These books are dangerous because they promote the kind of wishful thinking that leads to poor choices. For example, a person may *wish* to be an artist out of a hidden desire to avoid conformity. For that person, the artist's life is the antithesis of being ordinary. It makes them special, and thereby worthy of attention and love. For such a person, "art" is really a form of psychological rebellion.

Art is not the real issue behind their career choice. Even if this person decides to become an artist, he or she probably won't be satisfied. The person who decides to become an artist out of sincere love and appreciation for the activity itself, however, stands a much better chance. For that individual, art satisfies valid needs for creativity, meaningful work, and relating to society as a whole.

Defining the problem so that it addresses the real issues is the first step in eliminating wishful thinking from your decision process. One way of gauging the difference between wishful thinking and valid pursuit is to consider your own experiences in a historical sense. By looking at your "completed experiments," you can see what you were actually motivated to do. Wishful thinking, on the other hand, deals with *un*completed experiments that never come to fruition in reality.

> **By looking at your "completed experiments," you can see what you were actually motivated to do.**

In closing this chapter, I would like to leave you with one final thought. If you walk around with a problem, but never "deliver" it to your brain, you are limiting yourself. True, the emotional aspects of the problem define how you feel about it and what your needs are. But, once defined, your rational mind is the agent that can help you satisfy those needs.

Another way of saying this is: *Transform the problem into a goal.* When you restate the problem as a goal, it becomes much easier to sort through the possible paths to reach it, as we shall see in the next two chapters.

TRANSFORM THE PROBLEM INTO A GOAL

■ The problem states a situation in *negative* terms.

■ A goal states the situation in *positive* terms.

■ Problems typically are *general* and *pervasive*, with many subjective aspects and "loose strings."

■ A goal refers to *specific* and *concrete* actions that you will implement in the near future.

3

FIND AND CREATE
USEFUL ALTERNATIVES

HOW TO CREATE MORE OPTIONS FOR YOURSELF

Many effective business managers have a simple rule about subordinates bringing them problems: Don't bring me a problem without also bringing me possible solutions! This rule can be used to advantage in personal life. When it comes to your decisions, you are the manager. It's important not to saddle yourself with a problem without also considering ways to address it.

Alternatives are paths by which we can reach our goals. Even if two people have an identical goal, the paths they use to get there may be very different. The paths open to us depend on our unique personality, situation, and resources. For each of us, there are many paths, many ways to reach the goal, if we but take the time and energy to consider them. You can create more options for yourself by:

Brainstorming: Write down as many alternatives as come to mind. Do not censor or judge them at this stage. Even if these options seem wild to you, write them down. After all, if they have somehow popped into your mind, then there must have been something that prompted it. By looking at some of these wild options in ensemble, you may learn something about yourself. Perhaps they suggest that you should be doing more people-oriented work or that you value creative effort more than you acknowledge. By studying your wild guesses, you may be able to discern a useful pattern.

Brainstorming is most fruitful when it juxtaposes two familiar items to come up with a third item that is new. Creating analogies tends to stimulate this process. Thus, it's often useful to ask questions such as:

How is this like a game of chess?

How is this like a marriage?

How is this like a tool box?

How is this like Tom Peters?

Tim and I were brainstorming about how he should undertake a career transition. Tim had already attained great success in his field, but wanted a new challenge. He no longer wanted to be a professor; after thirty years, it was boring. He knew only that he had something worthwhile to say and that he wanted to bring his message to a larger audience.

I said, "How about becoming a consultant?"

Tim responded, "Too stressful."

I asked, "How about writing books on the subject?"

Tim said, "I already was doing that. It helps, but it doesn't get me to where I want to go."

"Okay," I said, "How about working for a major corporation as an executive or company guru?"

"Too cloistered and too political," Tim responded.

Finally, an intuitive flash came to me. I mentioned the name of a famous management expert who gave seminars on 'how things should be done'. Tim moved in his chair as if a jolt of electricity had gone through his body.

"Eureka! Yes! That's it!" Tim exclaimed, "Giving seminars is a way to reach my goal and bypass the shortcomings of the other options. Why didn't I think of that?"

At this creative stage in the process, let go of practical matters and give free reign to your imagination. Don't ask too many questions about where each option leads. The use of critical judgment at this stage eliminates many useful options before their real merit becomes apparent.

Asking other people: Others see you in a different light. Some may project their own values onto your situation, but if you ask a variety of people, you will doubtless get a good sampling of options. Chapter 8, though, will warn you about overdoing this technique. After considering other people's advice, you still have a responsibility to decide for yourself.

Making a list of options that other people have used: Look at what others in your situation have done. If certain options worked well for them, would they also work for you?

Combining other options: Take two not-quite-workable options and create a dual approach that captures the best features of each while minimizing the liabilities.

Playing what-if: Consider all the commitments in your life. These things may be holding you back more than you realize. Ask, "What if this job, marriage, parental responsibility, or mortgage were no longer in effect? What would I do then?"

Other what-if's that may unlock some new alternatives are: "What if I had a million dollars? What if my health were to change suddenly? What if I only had six months to live?"

The answers you generate may surprise you. You may be able to define alternatives you truly desire, but which you have automatically ruled out in the past. The option becomes open to you *if* you can figure out how to overcome the obstacle. Perhaps that obstacle is not as insurmountable as you have thought. Perhaps you have told yourself that there is no way you can overcome it—without really exploring whether that statement is true. From personal experience, I can tell you that obstacles become less intimidating as soon as you allow certain options to be recognized.

Listening better: Sometimes your clients, coworkers, boss, spouse, or children will offer you valuable insight into alternatives you never even considered. All it costs is the patience to listen.

Many years ago, I had an experience I will never forget. I was giving a presentation to some high-level managers in a large and prestigious electronics company. I was discussing a problem with getting a cooling unit for one of their special test rigs. The vendors who responded to the company's request to bid on the cooling unit had all quoted extremely high prices (over \$10,000) and delivery dates of three months. We had budgeted a much smaller amount of money and needed a delivery in two weeks. What were we to do? I made the casual comment that the vendors were holding us up, that all we needed was a water fountain cooler modified with a few extra lines and controls.

The custodian, who was in the conference room emptying the waste paper baskets, came over to me. He meekly tapped me on the shoulder and asked, "Could I please have a word with you outside?" He apologized for listening to our conversation, but thought he might be able to help. He had just finished a course on air conditioning and was sure he could do the job for us. Furthermore, he was rebuilding a water cooler in the custodian's shop and said that we could have it for our project.

Being the inquisitive type, I said, "Show me." He took me down into the bowels of the building. Sure enough, there was the water cooler and his latest tube-fitting project. He explained how he could easily modify the machine to suit our purposes. When I arrived back upstairs, I announced that we had another alternative. After a short deliberation, we decided that we had nothing to lose and everything to gain.

The custodian delivered the machine in two days and it worked perfectly! Our total cost was zero. As a footnote to this story, we later recommended the custodian for a distinguished service award given annually by the company. He was honored at a banquet and given a \$500 check.

Taking your mind OFF the problem: Sometimes, you can try too hard in coming up with alternatives. In such circumstances, your thoughts tend to fall into a rut that corresponds to rehashing the pros and cons repeatedly. If you find yourself in this situation, one way to get out is to relax and let your creative unconscious take over. When you are relaxed, alternatives will come naturally and when you least suspect them. Good ideas will just "happen" while you are in the shower, driving the car, listening to a concert, watching a movie, or exercising.

INCLUDE ALTERNATIVES THAT REFLECT YOUR GOALS AND VALUES

In *Freedom and Nature*, French philosopher Paul Ricoeur introduces a very useful notion for decision makers. Ricoeur says deciding is an intentional act. In making a decision, a person turns his or her self toward a *project*. He or she commits his or her self to certain actions to be done. Because the mind must project these acts into the future before they are actualized, in deciding, a person claims the project as his or her own. People hope their proposed actions will accomplish their purposes. In this sense, deciding is an activity that brings people closer to their goals.

The notion of a project allows you to examine the past evidence in your life with an eye toward extracting valuable information about motives that you actually enacted and completed. Using the concept of a project, you can examine the many small decisions already present in your everyday life. The evidence is already there, but the thread running through it, connecting isolated acts to an intelligible whole, may not yet have become obvious. By examining the evidence (smaller projects) in your life and asking, "To what end do they point?" you can gain a much better perception of your own values and motivations.

The concept of a project deemphasizes the moment of decision as the most critical in the process. In reality, we decide at each moment. The problem is that we are often not *aware* of the significance of these small decisions. In consciousness, we fail to connect these isolated acts to more powerful motives that swell within us.

The momentous decision to embark in a "new" direction may be the culmination of a long process in which we have already long focused psychic energies in less apparent ways. It is this building of energies—this investiture of the self into the project—that makes the human decision process unique.

The human decision process is mediated by the emotions. In deciding, I make a statement about myself, my identity, my values in the world. To decide is to *place* myself in the world.

Scientific decision processes, while valuable in many technical and business contexts, are lacking this human aspect. They are completely determinate in the sense that the values and alternatives are already chosen. These methods (often computerized) can calculate an exact ("optimum") way to allocate effort and resources for a given set of options and criteria. But because they cannot develop their own values and criteria, they are limited in an important way. The computer does not *care* about the choices it makes.

To decide is to *place* myself in the world.

Is skill at games like chess indicative of the ability to make decisions? Yes, but such abilities do not necessarily carry over into other areas of life. Games are different from ordinary life. They posit goals within a microcosm of predetermined rules, strategies, risks, and trade-offs. Because the game does not involve the whole of the player's identity, the way the player imputes himself into this project is fundamentally different from the way he makes real-life decisions. Games are for "fun," which is to say that the risk to self-esteem is limited. In playing a game, I lose awareness of my *self*. In recreation, I become anonymous. I do not have to place my unique self into the game.

Furthermore, skill is not the ultimate criterion in decision making. Just because you're good at something doesn't automatically mean you should pursue it:

> Herman Cohen taught his dog, Moishe, to stand on his hind legs for twenty minutes at a time. Then he taught the dog to wear a yarmulke, the prayer cap. Next Cohen got a prayer shawl and taught Moishe not to shrug it off his shoulders. When Moishe had mastered this, Cohen taught him how to daven [intone the Jewish prayers] along with the proper head motions.

> When the high holidays came, Cohen took Moishe with him to the synagogue. The dog handed the usher his ticket and sat down beside Cohen. At the right time, Moishe rose to pray, along with the rest of the congregation. True, his praying was not very clear, and was punctuated by muffled yips and heartfelt wails, but there was no doubt about it—the dog was praying.

> Mr. Shapiro, who was sitting on the other side of Moishe, exclaimed, "Herman, do my ears play tricks on me, or is your puppy actually davening?"

> "He's davening all right."

"Herman!" cried Shapiro. "You can make a fortune. This dog belongs on television!"

Sighed Herman, "Don't eat your heart out. *He* wants to be an accountant."

When it comes to listing alternatives, it helps not only to say who you are, but also who you are *not*. In committing to a particular action, a decision necessarily excludes other actions. Decisions *simplify* life by channeling energies and making you less divided. A decision removes an issue from the realm of conjecture (in which all options are possible) to the realm of unified action. The emotional energy previously used to display all options as equally possible is freed up when action is taken.

A decision to keep all your options open is not really a decision but a short-term tactic that is often misused. Keeping all options open in the deliberation process is useful, but once action has been initiated, some options must be discarded to focus fully on the chosen path.

Decisions *simplify* life by channeling energies and making you less divided.

It's important to realize that every decision implies with it not only a turning toward a goal, but also a turning away from other goals. Some things (be they material, social connections, habits, attitudes, freedoms, or fears) must be given up in order to support your decision. An inability to do this suggests that self-deception is in progress: You are attempting to eat your cake and have it too.

Making sure that your alternatives support your values involves some subtle issues. In the Introduction, I described a career decision in which I managed to avoid deciding on the real issue. I fooled myself into deciding on an issue that allowed me to "save" my bias. I had, in effect, already decided before I even entered the formal decision process of evaluating my alternatives!

I unconsciously ruled out the very alternative that would have supported my values. It required overcoming a fear of promoting my business more aggressively. I rejected that alternative because it violated an old prejudice that equated aggressiveness with being pushy and disrespectful of other people's rights. I didn't allow that I could have tried harder without stepping on people's toes. Further, I was afraid of trying. The net result was that I decided to decide on an issue that didn't matter, on one that didn't really solve the problem.

I used reverse gear and ran back to old, safe, familiar situations—instead of shifting to a different forward gear. My ego was not strong enough to withstand the criticism, resistance, and marketing competition that might have been encountered. So I posed myself two choices, neither of which were satisfactory. To sum up, I accepted the job that my decision matrix showed to be the best bet. Ten months later I quit!

I learned a valuable lesson from this. I needed to learn how to assert my needs in the face of opposition. To do this, I had to *unlearn* certain things I had learned as a young child: "Never assert yourself in the face of resistance." "Never fight for your rights." "Avoid competition and confrontation at all costs." These dictums became my hidden bias. They operated not only in employment situations, but in every aspect of my life. They explained why many of my other efforts were counterproductive.

Once I realized what I had been doing with my hidden bias, I was able to improve my decision making considerably. I started accessing aggressive energies. I learned to affirm the necessity of trying harder and accepting confrontation as part of the game. I learned to *feel* good about being aggressive in socially acceptable ways, such as self-promotion. Moreover, it seemed as though my will was getting stronger: It was a lot easier to say "No" when I knew I could back that answer up with suitably aggressive (or defensive) actions.

WHY WE OVERLOOK GOOD ALTERNATIVES

Biases and prejudices are hidden assumptions that can influence your decisions in a major way. Biases induce us to make the same choices consistently in many different contexts. They appear in the form of rules we tell ourselves:

DEVELOPING ALTERNATIVES

1. Write down **everything** that comes to mind. Do not censor your ideas at this point.

2. What do other people typically do to solve this problem?

3. Is there any benefit to doing nothing? Does ignoring the problem or developing better frustration tolerance provide a useful answer?

4. Can common strategies be **combined** to generate a solution?

5. What alternatives would have you doing what you would most like to do?

6. What alternatives use **unique talents** you possess in other areas of your life?

7. If you can't think of alternatives that solve the problem in a single step, are there ways to solve it in a short series of steps?

8. Include alternatives such as pursuing the present path more aggressively (or, for some people, less aggressively).

9. Consider alternatives in which you are **collaborating** with others to obtain resources and support that you cannot provide by yourself. (Lone Ranger thinking will take you only so far!)

10. Brainstorm with others. Every person sees you, your problem, and your alternatives--differently. Seeking out a wide range of advisors may help you discover additional **alternatives**.

1. Always play it safe.

2. Never speak your own mind.

3. Never trust a person who doesn't like beer, golf, baseball, . . .

4. Go for the job offering the most money or status.

5. Always back down when the going gets tough.

6. Insist that all your efforts have an instant payoff.

7. Never assert your own needs.

8. Never put yourself in a position where you can be rejected.

9. Never trust a woman/child/boss/person of different race or religion/. . .

10. Always play by the rules.

Biases in judgment can be picked out by critically examining your past decisions and looking for the threads of consistency and commonality. By examining your decisions, you may be able to see the presence of a repeated situation, scenario, fear, or anxiety that prompted you to act the way you did. Were you overreacting with catastrophe thinking? Were you underreacting by ignoring vital data? Were you consistently overestimating your own abilities? Were you consistently underestimating the resources required? Did you consistently misinterpret obvious messages? Did you consistently hesitate until the decision was made for you? Did you give up prematurely? Did you hold on too long?

DISCOVER YOUR DECISION-MAKING STYLE

We all have a unique decision-making *style*. Our biases cause us to approach most of our decisions in a consistent manner, even though the subject matter of the decisions may vary widely. Once you have discovered your decision-making style, it will be much easier to "lean" against your biases. You will be able to counteract, in a manner of speaking, your own personality.

In trying to understand your previous choices, you may see that certain psychological habits have made your decisions for you. Your "decisions" may actually be the results of old emotional patterns that sometimes defeat your own best interests. On an emotional level, you may be making the *same* decision over and over again!

Here is one way to gain some insight into your decision-making style. Make a list of past situations and events that made you happy. Jot down beside each entry the *feeling* that accompanied the event. Make another list of past events that made you unhappy, events that you wish had never happened. For this second list, also record the specific emotion that accompanied each event. Now, try to find the "emotional threads" that tie together the entries on these two lists. Is there a common theme or emotion that runs through them? Is there a general way that you approach problems, be they in your social, work, or family contexts?

For example, John considered his list of disappointing experiences. He saw that in both his personal and professional life, when the going got tough, his response was always the same: flight. He always escaped instead of trying harder, fighting, negotiating, or passively resisting. Sometimes this single method of response served him well. In other events, his habit of fleeing—quitting jobs and relationships at the first sign of resistance—had disastrous consequences. He acted on the basis of anticipated catastrophes that rarely materialized. He could run *away*, but often had nothing to run *to*. He did not have another sanctuary, friend, or job already lined up. His anxiety in the face of resistance or problems was so great that other ways of handling problems were not visible.

Underlying John's tendency to flee from problems was an overwhelming fear of rejection if he were to hold his ground rather than flee. This fear of rejection was so strong that he would even depart from a strongly desired situation to avoid any possibility of conflict, failure, or criticism. His anxiety, in effect, made decisions *for* him.

Both psychological perfectionism and its philosophical cousin, idealism, make decisions difficult. Both present criteria that rarely, if ever, can be satisfied. To perfectionists, *all* courses of action appear to have major faults and negative consequences. Perfectionists avoid action by searching for options in which they do not have to offend their highly developed moral conscience. As Sartre illustrated in his play, *Dirty Hands*, such options exist only in the perfectionist's mind, not in reality.

It is ironic that overly zealous pursuit of moral excellence should lead so directly to *paralysis* of effective action. At first examination, it seems that moral insight and high values would improve the quality of decisions. Yet, unbridled enthusiasm for a perfect solution in which everyone is benefited and no one loses—serves to detach one from the real world. Sometimes, the "should be" must take second seat to the "what is" in order to bring direction into our lives.

When standards are set too high, all realistic courses of action are rejected. Without relaxing the standards, the only options that can be embraced are the cop-outs. They ignore the real world and falsely insist that we can derive benefits without having to satisfy anyone else's needs. The way out of this dilemma is to relax the values and moral judgments that are creating this situation.

> # When standards are set too high, all realistic courses of action are rejected.

Reducing perfectionism widens the options. No longer must you search for the single option that optimizes status, beauty, convenience, safety, or financial return. Defining lofty and elusive alternatives can be a form of self-punishment that denies you the benefits of ordinary living! Setting realistic standards, on the other hand, allows you to trade openly with the real world to get the things you need. It is not an assault on your moral or spiritual integrity, but a mechanism that allows you to nourish yourself.

I have discussed perfectionism at length because it is one of the most common biases in decision making. The table entitled "Identify your Decision-Making Style" lists other biases. Each can dominate decision making to such a degree that it is appropriate to call them decision-making *styles*. The table also gives the telltale signs of each style and some ways to compensate for it. On the lighter side, it's entertaining to scan the list and see how aptly some descriptions fit friends, family members, and acquaintances. On the more serious side, the table will help you better assess your own style and compensate for it, resulting in a better decision-making process.

In later chapters, we will discuss biases in further detail and show how to counteract them with:

■ Assertiveness training

■ Self-promotion

■ Fair fighting

■ Affirmations

■ Reparenting

■ Risking more effectively

■ Paying the price

IDENTIFY YOUR DECISION-MAKING STYLE

STYLE	CHARACTERISTICS	WAYS TO COMPENSATE
The procrastinator	Always generates an excuse to put things off.	Force yourself to take first steps. Schedule important priorities.
The conservative	Feels uncomfortable trying new things or doing it someone else's way. Always plays it safe. Avoids risk, even at the expense of growth.	Affirm need for growth in specific areas. Learn the value of losing. (See Chapter 10.)
The impulsive	Responds without thinking through consequences.	Deliberately wait before reacting. Consider rationale and probable consequences.
The poll-taker	Is too dependent on other people's opinions.	Learn to value your own opinions and feelings.
The intellectualizer	Researches a decision to death, thereby postponing it. Concern with details and rationale prevents directly acknowledging desires and feelings.	Simplify the issues. Accept that decisions need not explain everything in order to be effective. Force yourself to action.
The hysteric	Is overwhelmed by common situations. Screams to be saved by others when self-initiated action is appropriate.	Assume personal responsibility. Improve frustration tolerance and self-assertiveness.
The sensitive	Has extreme concern with avoiding poverty, loneliness, or ridicule.	Consider if you can survive the worst possible outcome. Affirm your "right to lose" in the course of gaining your goals.

STYLE	CHARACTERISTICS	WAYS TO COMPENSATE
The dreamer	Waits for his or her ship to come in. Depends on magic, special signs, and astrology to indicate choices. Wishful thinking allows dreamer to ignore important facts.	Overcome emotional blocks to self-empower-ment. (See Chapter 11.) Develop plans that ac-knowledge give-and-take trading to get what you need.
The quitter	Withdraws after minor or momentary losses. Charlie Brown: "No problem is so small that it can't be run away from."	Summon aggressive ener-gies in pursuit of worthy goals. Try harder. Affirm talents. Confront anxiety over worst outcomes.
The alarmist	Always looking over their shoulder for imminent di-saster. Embraces all-or-nothing thinking: victory or castastrophe, nothing be-tween.	Reduce anxiety. Recognize that "always preparing for external crises" is a ploy to avoid acting on one's own goals.
The perfectionist	Sets self up for failure by taking steps that are too large. Is over-ambitious. Adopts standards too high to be realized.	Learn to moderate expec-tations. Acknowledge real needs instead of desire to be perfect, brilliant, or ex-ceptional.
The pleaser	Seeks approval at all costs and is easily humiliated by rejection. Sacrifices own goals and choices in order to gain or keep affections of others.	Place more weight on ob-jective criteria. Say "no" to situations contrary to own needs. Reduce inclination to embarrassment by taking self-assertive-ness course.
The loner	Fails to collaborate or de-velop support group. "I can do it all myself." Considers accepting help a sign of weakness.	Develop the humility and flexibility to accept help and advice from others. Seek counseling on issue of trust.

STYLE	CHARACTERISTICS	WAYS TO COMPENSATE
The manipulator	Ventures only if person has complete control or power of veto. Acts without regard for others affected by the decision.	Recognize value of including others in win-win situations. Watch movie version of Dickens's *A Christmas Carol.*
The status seeker	Is too concerned with prestige, money, or looks—and not enough with how he or she really feels about the activity itself.	Pay special attention to all other criteria that determine an option's suitability. (See Chapter 4.)
The optimist	Does not consider liabilities carefully enough. Overestimates own abilities.	Have others advise you about major obstacles and stumbling blocks. Then make a plan that will address them. (Details are in Chapter 5.)
The pessimist	Overestimates the height of obstacles. Underestimates his or her own abilities and resources that can be utilized.	Accept obstacles as part of life and then overcome them with confidence. Affirm own abilities.
The opportunist	Considers only short-term benefits and fails to account for significant long-term effects.	Visualize long-term goals and put them in writing. Read Chapter 7 on evaluating opportunities.

4

MAKE TRADE-OFFS YOU
CAN LIVE WITH

HOW TO EVALUATE ALTERNATIVES

In Chapter 2, the problem-solving aspect of decisions was introduced. Formulating the decision as a problem is a necessary step in cutting the decision down to size. Without it, we would be overwhelmed by its complexity or would spend too much time gathering information.

The figure "Three-Step Problem-Solving Process" (next page) shows the process for solving a problem once it has been defined. The first step, generating alternatives, was discussed in Chapter 3. This chapter deals with the second and third steps.

The second step is to determine how well each alternative actually solves the problem. It is a *criteria filter*. All alternatives are measured to find the ones that satisfy your needs, constraints, and values.

THREE-STEP PROBLEM-SOLVING PROCESS

PROBLEM

```
┌─────────────────────────────────┐
│  1. GENERATE ALTERNATIVES       │
│     What are my choices?         │
└─────────────────────────────────┘

┌─────────────────────────────────┐
│  2. CONSIDER CRITERIA            │
│     Will it solve the problem?   │
└─────────────────────────────────┘

┌─────────────────────────────────┐
│  3. DETERMINE FEASIBILITY        │
│     Will it work in the real world? │
└─────────────────────────────────┘
```

SOLUTION

If *no* alternatives emerge after step 3, repeat the process, and

■ *Generate more alternatives.* (Do creative visualizations, ask friends for suggestions, seek advice of professionals, do more research, etc.)

■ *Relax the criteria.* (Moderate your expectations and standards so as to become unstuck. This is especially relevant for those with "perfectionist" decision-making styles.)

■ *Seek ways to improve the feasibility of your alternatives.* (Can you borrow resources, modify the conditions, collaborate with others, or combine existing alternatives?)

This criteria filter, however, says nothing about whether you will be able to attain your goal or whether the world will be receptive to your decision. Thus, one more critical step is needed: a *feasibility filter*. It asks, "Will this alternative work in the real world?" The feasibility filter is used *after* the criteria filter for reasons of efficiency. The second step takes relatively little time, but evaluating feasibility can be a lengthy process.

Now let's look at the second and third steps in more detail.

DEVELOP YOUR OWN CRITERIA

Criteria help you answer the question, "What constitutes a solution to this problem?" There are two general categories of criteria in most decisions, the *must-haves* and the *wants*. For example, a person considering several job offers may set their must-haves as a minimum salary of $40,000 per year and a maximum commuting distance of 30 miles.

Each must-have criterion should be phrased so that it can be answered with a clear "yes" or "no." In the above example, each prospective job offer will either meet the minimum salary figure or it will not. If a *must-have* cannot be stated in this unambiguous way, chances are that it belongs in the *wants* column.

The function of this criteria sift is to prevent you from choosing alternatives that do not meet your basic needs. Alternatives that do not satisfy your must-have criteria almost always turn sour, because they are not solutions to the problem in the first place.

Be realistic in setting your must-have criteria. Do you *absolutely* need to earn that much money? Must your prospective spouse *absolutely* have a movie-star appearance? Must the house you intend to purchase *absolutely* have a swimming pool? If your must-haves are too numerous or ambitious, you may be ruling out many acceptable and useful alternatives before you've had a chance to consider their overall merit.

On the other hand, appropriate must-haves should always be included. They ensure that the really important aspects of the decision will not be ignored. The must-have criteria serve an important checking function. It's too easy to deceive yourself with ranking methods if you have not already filtered out choices that clearly don't solve the problem or support your values!

You have a lot more freedom with the *wants*. You simply specify the characteristics that are important, but that do not fall into the must-have category. For personal decisions, limit your want list to ten items. Listing more than this is distracting. (If you have more than ten, try to combine the similar items and drop the frivolous or minor ones.)

Alternatives that do not satisfy your MUST-HAVE criteria almost always turn sour because they are not solutions to the problem in the first place.

The table "Typical Criteria" (page 51) shows one person's criteria for three common decisions. The first column gives the must-haves and wants for selecting a suitable spouse. (Of course, these are for illustration purposes only. In real life, we do not walk around with such a list trying to find a match!) The value of making such a list is that it provides some standards for when we *do* meet people face to face. The person who made this list doesn't have to consider dating someone who is a drug addict, for example. They *already* know that such a person is unsuitable, no matter how attractive the person's other qualities may be.

Similarly, in the second column, the job seeker has determined that he doesn't want to relocate, period. Knowing this saves time in searching for a job that *does* satisfy the requirements.

Once you have set your criteria, it's time to look at your list of alternatives. The chart "Find Alternatives that Meet Your Criteria" (on page 52) is a worksheet that will help you do this. The goal of filling in this worksheet is to narrow down your list of alternatives. First, list the criteria you have developed above on the left side of the worksheet. Second, list the alternatives (A through E or however many you have) you are considering for this decision. Third, for each alternative, ask yourself whether each must-have is satisfied. Put a "Yes" or "No" in the indicated space. After this is done, *eliminate* those alternatives that do not meet your must-have criteria. These alternatives simply do not solve the problem.

TYPICAL CRITERIA

For Prospective Spouse	For Job Hunting	Buying an Office Copier
MUST HAVES:		
1. No drug addicts	Minimum acceptable salary	Fast and convenient service
2. No alcoholics	Does not require relocation	Price
3. Not already married		
WANTS:		
1. Good looks	Advancement	Performance
2. Intelligence	Commuting distance	Operating costs
3. Kindness	Interesting work	Reliability
4. Compatible life-style	Benefits	Ease of use
5. Healthy	Nice people environment	Low noise
6. Sexually compatible	Security	Durability
7. Responsible	Responsibility	Upgrade compatibility
8. Compatible values	Autonomy	
9. Sense of humor	Enough free time for family	
10. Makes me feel good	Agrees with my values and goals	

Next, look at the list of wants for each option. Rate each want on the list from 1 to 10, depending on the degree to which it is satisfied (10 = complete satisfaction). Finally, add the total wants score for each alternative. The option with the highest score is the best match to your criteria. However, don't be too anxious to "choose" it at this stage. The purpose of this technique is merely to throw out the bad apples and the not-so-good apples. One more important consideration remains.

FIND ALTERNATIVES THAT MEET YOUR CRITERIA

CRITERIA	ALTERNATIVES				
	A	B	C	D	E
MUST-HAVES:					
1.					
2.					
3.					
WANTS:					
1.					
2.					
3.					
4.					
5.					
6.					
7.					
8.					
9.					
10.					
TOTAL					

For each MUST-HAVE, respond with a YES or NO. For each WANT, rank the alternatives A to E (or however many alternatives you have) from 1 to 10, based on the degree to which they satisfy that WANT (10 = complete satisfaction). Add the total numerical WANTS score for each alternative.

HOW FEASIBLE ARE YOUR ALTERNATIVES?

So far, you have weeded out alternatives that do not meet *your* needs and criteria. What remains is to figure out how your proposed actions will be received by *the world*. The feasibility filter does exactly this. It evaluates the likelihood that you can successfully carry out your decision. Feasibility depends on many factors. Some of these are internal, such as your abilities, attitudes, resources, and desire for the goal. Others are external, such as market conditions, the amount of competition, and conflicting demands on your time and energy. All these factors can be grouped into five general categories:

EFFECTIVENESS: What is the probability of success? Will this alternative bring results in a suitable time frame? Are external conditions favorable? Can I obtain the resources needed?

EFFICIENCY: Is this an efficient use of my time, energy, and talent? Are there better ways to reach the same goal?

DIRECTION: Is this a step in the right direction? Is it compatible with my long-range plans? Is it compatible with long-term market trends?

RECOVERY: Can I recover if this alternative proves intractable? What is the worst that could happen? Do I have a fall-back position?

COMPLETENESS: Will reactions from family, friends, coworkers, or community impact the outcome? Have I considered how to handle their probable responses? Have I accounted for the existence of competition? What other contingencies might significantly reduce my ability to carry out this alternative?

The chart "Evaluate the Feasibility of Your Alternatives" (on page 54) is a self-quiz that simplifies this step of the process. After completing it, you'll have a good sense for the *overall* feasibility of each alternative. (Some items may need to be rephrased to apply to your particular decision.) There are no passing or failing grades in this feasibility quiz. What's important is the *relative* score of the alternatives. However, scores below 35 would suggest a feasibility problem, considering your present abilities, resources, and situation. I would not discourage you from that alternative, especially if your heart is set on it! All it says is that you may need to take intermediate steps to develop resources or improve your situation before committing yourself fully.

EVALUATE THE FEASIBILITY OF YOUR ALTERNATIVES

CONSIDERATION	POINTS	A	B	C
1. I have the ability to do it.	15			
2. I have the resources, time, money, contacts, and credentials to do it.	15			
3. I can withstand some setbacks along the way.	5			
4. The "market conditions" are favorable.	10			
5. I can manage conflicting demands.	5			
6. I have persistence and strong desire for the goal.	15			
7. This alternative provides an efficient way to reach my goal.	5			
8. This alternative is a step in the right direction and is compatible with my long-term plans.	5			
9. I have an acceptable fall-back position in case the worst happens.	10			
10. The worst outcome, if it did happen, would not be unbearable to me.	5			
11. I have considered probable reactions from friends, family, coworkers, and community—and know how to address them	10			
TOTAL	100			

For alternatives A, B, and C, respond to each consideration with a number score. Give yourself the maximum number of points indicated in the points column if you strongly agree, or if the statement is completely true for that alternative. Give yourself proportionally fewer points, to the extent that you disagree with the statement. Add the totals for each alternative.

DECISION TREES CLARIFY THINKING
ABOUT OUTCOMES

Constructing a decision tree can be helpful in *thinking* about feasibility. (See the figure "The Decision Tree" on page 56 for an example based on choosing between two similar software packages.) In *acting* on the decision tree, you are free to back down from one branch and try another or to try two branches simultaneously. The value of a decision tree is that it sequences your actions in correct order, thereby minimizing the possibility of painting yourself into a corner.

The decision tree spells out where each alternative leads. (Notice that "Do nothing" and "Maintain status quo" are also usually options.) The decision tree shows the range of possible outcomes, usually in terms of "best-typical-worst" or "success-draw-failure." You also can indicate on it, in nutshell form, the resources needed for each branch. The decision tree clarifies how this decision meshes with your long-range plans. It forces you to make contingency plans and to consider the possibility that certain solutions may create problems worse than the original one.

Carrying the decision tree out to the second branch allows you to anticipate and compensate for problems that otherwise might be overlooked. That is, sometimes a victory can lead directly to a subsequent failure. Sometimes, a failure can unwittingly lead to a subsequent victory. Filling in the second branch is like looking ahead two moves in chess. It gives you an advantage in solidifying successes already won and in salvaging the most from losses encountered along the way.

TRADE-OFFS RESOLVE CONFLICTING VALUES

French philosopher Paul Ricoeur maintains that we experience decisions on four levels: the *event* that prompts the decision, the *project* (actions or responses) that the decision considers, the *values* that underlie the project, and the *self* that embraces these values. The order of these levels is one of decreasing visibility. Events are usually the most visible because they occur in the external world. Projects are less visible because it is often difficult to comprehend the purposes behind a series

THE DECISION TREE

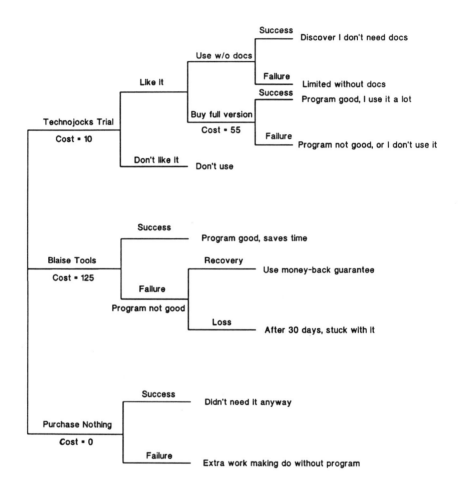

of actions. Values require even more scrutiny before they become apparent, even to ourselves. The self, paradoxically, is almost invisible to consciousness. (It is inextricably tied up in the task of being conscious!)

Events are things happening "out there" in the environment. From a psychological point of view, it is important to appreciate that some events are more powerful than others. A minor event will not deter you from the project at hand, but serves merely as an obstacle. For example, suppose the event is that you encounter a traffic jam on the way home. You can overcome this obstacle simply by taking an alternate route. Your project of getting home remains intact.

Sometimes, though, the event may be significant enough to force you to question the project. For example, if you have an accident on the way home and injure yourself, it would be wise to give up the project of going home and go to the hospital instead.

Events of yet larger impact can pull you back two levels, to questioning your values. For example, if a trusted family member or friend brutally attacks you, you might well question the values of trust and friendship that you have held over the years. The Book of Job is interesting in this respect. It suggests that there is one important exception to this rule: *No* event is potent enough to cause a person to reject his or her belief in God. The world crashed around Job. Most of us, if subjected to the same experiences, would give up our belief. The fact that Job still believed provides an inspiring model of religious faith.

Finally, traumatic events can pull you back three levels, to questioning your self. For example, consider the prisoner of war who is being brainwashed. After a certain amount of this treatment, the prisoner's self disintegrates. The prisoner no longer knows who he is or what he should do.

Having made these definitions, let's look more carefully at values. What are they, anyway? In the present context, values are thoughts suggesting rules of behavior:

> "Don't steal."
> "Show respect toward others."
> "Be honest."
> "Be loving to your children."
> "Find meaningful work."

It is significant that values take the imperative form. When a value is ours, we do not state it in factual or conditional terms, but as a *demand* for action.

The values underlying our decisions are not fixed and immutable mandates inherited from our parents, but evolve as we experience life. There is a dialectical relationship between values and experience. The famous German philosopher Immanuel Kant was mistaken in trying to deduce moral values from a priori principles (that is, from principles requiring no experience in the world). Values do not arise spontaneously from pure rational thought, but within the contexts of our accidental place in history and society. Further, the ensemble of values we accumulate in this fashion is not necessarily consistent, but forms a jumble in which individual values are often either contradictory or incommensurate.

The significance of this to practical decision making is immense: You cannot *decide* to change your values instantaneously. That is like saying you will yourself to become another person. Your values are a part of your consciousness that cannot be changed by mere will.

Values can be modified only indirectly. By placing the questioned value in brackets and devising experiments, you can see for yourself if that value is too restrictive. The resulting experiences eventually will modify or reaffirm that value without any conscious effort on your part. This pragmatic approach requires only the knowledge of how to conduct valid experiments and the courage to be open to the observed results.

Making sure that your actions support your values is a very important part of decision making. If a decision is difficult because it highlights a conflict within your constellation of values, then some method of resolution is needed. The *trade-off* is one such mechanism. It compromises one or more of your values in situations demanding decisive action.

There is no rational basis for trade-offs; they indicate how you—as the individual who must decide in your specific situation—*feel* about the relative merit of the conflicting values. Trade-offs are challenging because they are always made between apples and oranges, incommensurate factors that can never be objectively compared. You can never be totally certain of such subjective judgments. The best you can hope for is attaining the confidence that in making them, you are exercising your overall best option.

> A man walked into a pub, trailing an extremely foul odor behind him. He sat in a corner all alone. All evening he sat there nursing his beers. Finally, a woman at the bar felt so sorry for him that she held her nose and went over to his table.
>
> "Yes," he said, "it's always like this; I'm always alone. Nobody talks to me, nobody even comes near me, because of the smell. It's my job at the circus. I pick up the droppings behind the elephants, and the stench is awful. I have no friends and my life is terribly lonely."
>
> "In that case," she asked, "why don't you quit your job?"
>
> "What!" gasped the man. "And give up showbiz?"

The trade-off *integrates* separate parts to allow the whole to function more harmoniously. The fact that a decision is made possible this way does not take away its element of risk or the mixed feelings that may accompany it. The sacrifice of a secondary value in realizing a primary one may evoke considerable anguish. The redeeming quality counteracting this pain is the understanding that it leads to more satisfying compromises. This understanding emerges with clarity only after experiencing the frustration of trying to maintain two or more incompatible goals without compromising any of them.

Making trade-offs is the most stressful part of the decision process because it calls for honesty in examining motives. Some of our motives may be less ideal than the values we consciously profess. Integrity in decision making insists that we sometimes give up, or substantially modify, a value previously considered inviolate. This is difficult for those who think that it is always possible to find *some* way in which nothing has to be given up. Many positive-thinking books can be misleading in this regard. They can easily convince you that there is an easy way out, a way that keeps all the benefits while eliminating all the liabilities.

The trade-off *integrates* separate parts to allow the whole to function more harmoniously.

In particular, trying to "decide" your way out of long-standing employment, marriage, or social problems can create anxiety if you expect those decisions to eliminate *all* the negatives in your life. Expecting a single new alternative to resolve suffering in every aspect of your life is unrealistic. Most decisions can be optimized only with respect to their primary context, leaving the other contexts in need of additional decisions.

Choosing means *limiting* yourself. By committing yourself to a particular course of action, you are automatically ruling out certain other possibilities. A trade-off is painful because it is a reflection of our limitations as human beings. We cannot be all things to all people, especially to ourselves.

Because so many decisions depend on trade-offs, the quality of a decision is directly affected by the quality of the supporting trade-offs. To this extent, decision making is improved by increasing awareness of values and priorities on both conceptual and feeling levels. Especially on the feeling level, some motives remain hidden from consciousness, so that decisions seem to "happen" to us. We're never quite sure why we do certain things. When important motives are unconscious, they can bypass the entire decision process. In effect, these unconscious motives constitute a decision that has *already* been made. When these motives become conscious, we're more able to reason and feel our way through to a real decision.

If none of your alternatives seems acceptable, it's sometimes beneficial to turn the decision process on its head. Ask what values, if relaxed, would allow a solution to be found. Sometimes, the best decision is to do nothing at all—except increase your ability to tolerate frustration. This option is useful in complex situations from which you are nevertheless receiving significant benefits.

Trade-offs are painful because they reflect our human limitations. We cannot be all things to all people, especially to ourselves.

A SIMPLE METHOD FOR MAKING TRADE-OFFS

The amazing thing about trade-offs is that we *already* possess the knowledge to make them with great accuracy. For example, consider a trade-off between working environment and salary. How much salary would you sacrifice in order to work in an environment that was very pleasant? How much extra salary ("combat pay") would you require to work in a high-pressure environment or one that posed risk to your personal safety? I'll bet you can easily quantify these numbers.

In practice, trade-offs are not as simple because more than two factors (salary versus environment) are usually involved. In more complex situations, you will need to distill the decisional situation into the underlying values before you can arrive at a trade-off.

The figure "Making Trade-offs" on page 62 shows the six steps required. Under each step, in smaller type, are the details for a trade-off that Mary is considering. In this example, Mary is deciding whether to spend the next year writing a book on a subject that interests her or to continue working at a moderately pleasant job that provides financial security. If she spends the next year writing, there is the risk that the book may never be accepted for publication. Even if it is accepted, there is additional risk that it may earn less income than expected. On the other hand, if she spends the next year working for her employer, she is financially secure, but unfulfilled in developing an important goal.

In the first step, Mary lists the advantages and disadvantages of each option. In the second step, she distills each option into its underlying, or basic, value. In her case, the trade-off is between financial security and personal fulfillment. She is considering, "Would I trade X dollars of income for Y amount of opportunity to write a book?" (Other basic trade-offs are status versus practicality, autonomy versus relationship, and safety versus growth.)

The third step is to find the *balance point*. That is, how much X is worth a given amount of Y? Most people find that they have a good feel for it. Imagine a linear scale between the extremes of all-X and all-Y. For example, in Mary's case, at one extreme, there is much security working at her job, but little

MAKING TRADE-OFFS

1. **LIST** advantages and disadvantages for each option.

MARY'S TRADEOFF

OPTION A: Remain at Present Job   OPTION 2: Write Book

Advantages   Advantages
  a. Financial Security   a. Personal Fulfillment
  b. Pleasant Working Environment   b. Opportunity
Disadvantages   Disadvantages
  a. Work not meaningful   a. Risk of failure
  b. Lack of autonomy   b. Social Isolation

2. **DISTILL** each option into its underlying value.

Security   vs.   Fulfillment

3. **FIND** the balance point.

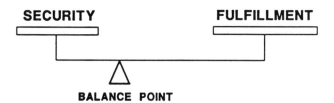

SECURITY   **FULFILLMENT**

BALANCE POINT

For Mary, fulfillment is twice as important as security. The balance point is 1/3 security and 2/3 fulfillment.

4. **SEE** where conditions lie with respect to the balance point.

Money: favorable   Ability: favorable   Market: favorable

5. **CHOOSE** the option on the favorable side.

Write the book!

6. **MANAGE** post-decisional anxiety and regret.

Mary resolved not to regret losing seniority and promotion possibilities at her old job. She developed a contingency plan to get professional editing help if the book took longer than planned.

fulfillment. At the other extreme, she finds much fulfillment in writing, but little financial security.

The amazing thing about trade-offs is that we ALREADY possess the knowledge to make them with great accuracy.

You find the balance point by asking, "At what point do I feel *indifferent* to the result?" Risking 50 percent of your security may make you uncomfortable in pursuing something as nebulous as "fulfillment." Yet, risking at the 10 percent level may be so painless that you would always be worrying that you had not tried hard enough to become fulfilled. For each individual situation, there is a unique point on the scale at which the decision becomes indifferent to the X versus Y issue. In the example, at the point of one-third security and two-thirds fulfillment, Mary felt that the tug of war reached a standstill.

Discovering the balance point is not the same as reaching a decision, but allows you to factor your values correctly into the whole of the decision. Step 4 evaluates the larger context with respect to the balance point. If the situation lies on one side of the balance point, the decision goes to X; if it lies on the other side, the decision goes to Y.[1]

In Mary's case, some of these conditions involved financial resources, level of confidence in her ability to complete the book, the publishing market at the time of completion, desire to do that project, the expected rewards for a successful effort, the probable penalties for failing, and her ability to manage the anxieties attending each alternative.

---

[1] I was once asked at a decision seminar, "What happens if both sides are exactly equal?" The answer: First, ask questions that further elucidate the differences between the two options and how you evaluate them. Second, examine your decision-making style and compensate for it (as described in Chapter 3). If you usually underestimate your abilities and resources, go with the higher-risk side. If you tend to overestimate your own ability or resources, go with the side of restraint.

For Mary, conditions were favorable. She had recently received an inheritance that amounted to a year's living expenses. She had already queried ten publishers and found three who stated strong interest in her project. She was reasonably certain she could finish the book in one year. The conditions lay on the side of writing the book. Thus in step 5, Mary chose to write the book. (Had the inheritance not appeared then, she might have been more reluctant to take the risk.)

Step 6 is to manage postdecisional regret and anxiety. These feelings usually follow a trade-off, because one of your important values is being compromised. Regret occurs when you must acknowledge lost opportunities on the path you are leaving. Anxiety occurs when you experience setbacks and obstacles on the newly chosen path. After the decision has been made, we sometimes forget the emotional price we have to pay for it.

Three months after Mary decided to write the book, her boss also left. Had she stayed, she would have been promoted to a position with considerably greater autonomy and creativity. Moreover, a year after she started, the book was accepted, but only on the condition that she revise it completely. This took an additional four months that she had not anticipated. Although she made a good decision, Mary needed to prepare herself for these disappointments and lost opportunities. Chapter 10 will discuss specific ways to deal with them.

A closing note on Mary's trade-off: A year after her book was published, the president of a large company read it and was so impressed by Mary's ability that he offered her a job that was twice as good as the one she had forfeited by leaving her old company.

5

OVERCOME OBSTACLES

DON'T LET FEARS HOLD YOU BACK

When you're first presented with an obstacle, fear magnifies it. You feel, "Perhaps I'm not smart enough, capable enough, or aggressive enough to reach the goal." These fears rekindle emotions originating from early childhood, in which you feel helpless and without the power to initiate action. As a result, the obstacle becomes larger and more ominous than it really is.

Once you accept your fears, it becomes easier to view the *structure* of the obstacle in detail and find ways to bypass it, attack it at its weakest point, or approach it differently. On an emotional level, the obstacle is cut down to size by *seeing* it as negotiable in small steps rather than as a huge monolithic hurdle that must be jumped in a single bound.

Thinking about the problem posed by the obstacle often does not solve it, but may only amplify your fears. In a subtle way, thought becomes sidetracked into worry, in which you wrestle with the fears instead of the goals.

Wrestling with the fears can *always* be justified. The fears relate to your survival needs, which cannot be ignored. More often than not, however, the fears capture *all* attention, effectively preventing action of any kind.

Excessive thinking about the problem has a snowball effect on the emotions. Instead of solving the problem, thinking about it makes it larger and more inertial, so that you feel less in control. The principle operating here is the *law of fear*: By paying attention to your fears, they become amplified.

It is proper to acknowledge your fears, but in the final say, you must act in spite of them. If you wrestle with the fears instead of the goals, progress becomes impossible. To wrestle with the fears—to try to satisfy their demands—only adds momentum to the rolling snowball.

Fear holds you back. It does not allow you to live totally. It keeps you divided. It leads to half-hearted efforts and fragmentary solutions. Strangely enough, people are *hypnotized* by their prior failures and rejections. In their trance, they cannot see any positive or constructive courses of action. They use exaggerated thinking and "cognitive deletion" to avoid courses of action that impose any risk, however minor, of suffering the intense emotions that caused the trance in the first place.

A common defense against obstacles is to *run* in the other direction. In escaping, you avoid the feared situation, but at the same time, you enter a new situation with problems all its own. Fleeing at the first sign of resistance is an implicit choice, one that embraces a new alternative without first forming the underlying commitment. When resistance is encountered again, these subsequent alternatives will also be abandoned. Without commitment to your chosen options, any and all obstacles will tend to throw you off the track.

According to the inimitable Charlie Brown, "No problem is so small that it can't be run away from." While we can all appreciate the humor in this, as a real-life policy, it's neurotic. The pain we suffer by facing our problem is *not* always worse than the compromises produced by running away. Refusing to face our problems leads to inaction, to excuse making, to distraction with mindless activities, and to drowning of awareness in drink or drugs. The fear of doing poorly can prevent us from accepting the important challenges that lie before us. When we withdraw from these challenges, we limit ourselves. We settle for less. We become less.

The *Law of Fear:* Paying attention to your fears makes them larger.

SIX WAYS TO OVERCOME OBSTACLES

Overcoming obstacles is one form of *learning.* Most people have a curiosity and a need to understand the obstacles facing them. They are not afraid to look at what blocks their movement. Neurotic individuals, however, would rather stifle their learning than gaze at certain favorite fears and self-limiting rules. Neurotics often display great resistance or inability to learn anything new. Because they are stuck in old and rigid ways of responding, they can't adapt to solve the new problems facing them. They prefer to suffer in a negative, but familiar, situation than to risk for what they really want.

The first step in dealing with obstacles is to view them in perspective. To determine their significance to your decision, ask yourself, "What is the worst that can happen? Can you live with this consequence? What is the probability that you will actually meet the obstacle? In contrast to the worst case, what *typically* might happen? Can you live with that?" In answering these questions, you provide *limits* to the fears generated by the obstacle and—in effect—cut the obstacle down in size.

Try to see the detailed structure of the obstacle. What specific aspects of this obstacle can be addressed individually? What can you change to remove the obstacle or get around it? Would you be willing to do that? How have other people gotten around this obstacle? Can you use their methods?

Look for changes that cope with, or adapt to, the obstacle. What actions will put it off into the future, refute it, encourage others to handle it for you, or reduce its impact?

STRATEGIES FOR OVERCOMING OBSTACLES

- **Fight:** Overcome them with superior strength.

- **Evasion:** Go around them.

- **Subversion:** Undermine them.

- **Alliance:** Gain help to resist.

- **Insulation:** Avoid their zone of influence.

- **Endurance:** Wait for them to go away or lose their power.

- **Rally:** Gain courage by celebrating prior successes.

Consider the resources needed to overcome or go around the obstacle. Describe them in detail. Can you find, earn, learn, invent, beg, borrow, or steal them? (It's reasonable to expect that you must give up something of worth to gain these resources.)

In particular, lack of money is often considered a major obstacle. We use it as an excuse for not acting upon our goals. I don't accept this excuse. In most cases, people who can't manage their money can't manage their minds.

Money problems are often just a metaphor for more general problems of self-esteem. Wherever we are on the income scale, we're much less likely to view lack of money as an obstacle if we feel secure about ourselves. Without self-esteem, we spend too much time looking for the easy way, for the risk-free way, for the way that bypasses hard work and sacrifice. With self-esteem, we can tolerate such inconveniences. We know that the goal is worth it, that *we* are worth it, and that we are strong enough to exert the effort.

FOCUS ON GOALS, NOT OBSTACLES

In my experience helping others with decision making, I have noticed that many people stop focusing on their goals as soon as they meet obstacles. Instead of spending their emotional energy on moving toward the goal, they use it to attack themselves and question their own worth.

It is amazing how some people see *only* the intractability of the system when they are "down." They feel victimized. They become totally unconscious of the fact that they have become passive. They are paralyzed from effective action by the hypnotic chains that bind them.

When some people are feeling down, all they can see is the intractability of the system.

When people are down, "deciding" can become an exercise in masochism. People in this situation beat themselves up with doubts, self-recriminations, self-pity, and questions about the accuracy of their observations. They say that they don't have enough money to do what they want, that they feel like they don't belong, and that they aren't sure how to interpret their situation. They jump to the conclusion that these "shortcomings" are their own fault. That is, they turn their decision problem into a form of self-torture. The language they use to themselves is self-accusatory and self-blaming. The anticipation of shame keeps them in a prison of doubt.

As psychiatrist Dr. Theodore Isaac Rubin notes in *Compassion and Self-Hate* (see Suggested Reading List) when people say "I should have known better" or "I was a fool for having tried that," they unconsciously believe that they should be perfect in their judgment, that they should not have to make any mistakes. They consciously punish themselves for the unconscious belief that they should be infallible. They experience emotional starvation and feelings of disappointment, rage, and impotence at their misfortune. These same people use their past mistakes, however trivial, as proof that they are not good enough or that they should have tried harder, and thereby turn their negative feelings onto themselves.

Self-hating people feel that they should give perfect performances, that they should make perfect decisions. As a result, self-hate leads to reluctance to make decisions, for all decisions carry an element of failure. Compassion for oneself reduces this element by allowing us to make imperfect decisions, by letting us maintain our self-esteem when we make errors. In fact, only when we allow ourselves to make *real* choices (choices that carry some element of risk) and to state what we prefer, do we generate self-esteem. Saying, "I want this, I am willing to face certain obstacles to gain it," is an existential expression of our self-worth.

If self-blaming people could be compassionate to themselves instead, they would accept their own fallibility as human. They would admit that learning involves making mistakes and poor judgments in a continuous process of development. Rubin emphasizes that the key to this acceptance is not intellectually grasping this principle, but emotionally realizing your own worth and learning to be compassionate to yourself.

People who have little self-esteem are often compelled to all-or-nothing thinking. They can't compromise or find the middle way in setting their goals. Compromise is viewed as threatening to their inner self: If I can't do it "my way" (translate: without psychological resistance of any kind), then I don't want it (translate: my weak ego can't manage it).

I feel there is a lesson in all of this: Learn to accept handling problems as part of life. There is no shortage of problems; the best we can do is become adept at handling them. This is what decision making is all about. It helps you solve problems and address needs in a way that lets you move on with your life. If you have the notion that decision making *eliminates* problems, then you will build up the unrealistic expectation that the goal is to have no problems. Decisions replace old problems with new problems. A more appropriate goal is being equal to your problems and not letting them prevent you from doing the things you need to do.

Decisions replace old problems with new problems.

SIDESTEP THE HURDLE OF UNREALISTIC EXPECTATIONS

It's reasonable to expect a career decision to satisfy your income needs. To expect that single career decision to provide all your other needs—relationship, romance, exercise, spirituality, and so on—is totally unreasonable. To be sure, these areas may be affected by your work decision, but it is wishful thinking to expect that a good career move will force these other concerns to fall into place.

The person who seeks the single decision that resolves *all* their problems is punishing themselves. They are looking for something that doesn't exist. Life insists that you sometimes make decisions in separate spheres, based on how your needs in those areas are being met. Looking for the single "magic solution" is a form of evasion and procrastination.

In considering a divorce, for example, it would be foolhardy to expect that once your marriage partner has gone, your life will instantly become fulfilled. Even if you have lined up some very attractive replacements, there is no way to know in advance whether they will be suitable. Divorce counselors tell their clients, "Don't expect to meet Mister or Miss Perfect as soon as you are divorced. Instead, expect lonely nights, disappointments in dating again, and some new compromises in settling down with another partner."

Whatever the situation, maintaining unrealistic expectations is dangerous to your emotional well-being. It leads to anxiety and poor relations with others, because it often means you are hoping to receive something they are not inclined to give.

By and large, if people value what you offer them, they will pay you (in some form). If they don't find value in it, they'll ignore or refuse your offer. Most of the time, there is a trade: You pay others and they, in turn, offer something of value to you. To consult with a doctor, you pay her. To get groceries, you pay the grocer. To take a dancing lesson with a dance instructor, you pay him. You trade your money for their merchandise or time (or vice versa). I mention these obvious facts only as a reminder: Be wary of basing important plans on schemes that elevate you while offering little value or motivation to others.

Writers, artists, musicians, and other creative types often fall into this trap. They love their activity so much that they put all their "emotional energy eggs" into one basket. They strike a bargain that the world has not really agreed to: They will dedicate themselves to working very hard, and the world will reward them with a larger than average payoff.

Creative people in this situation ignore financial reality. They rationalize, "Just because I love this activity, the world should shower me with recognition and money. After all, Pablo Picasso and James Michener made millions, so I'm not dreaming." When such expectations are not met with validation from the world, the creative person becomes anxious. ("Is the world blind to my great talents?") Wishful thinking has allowed them to confuse *what is* for *what they want*.

There is a practical solution for creative people struggling with this issue. The idea is not to abandon the activity, or even the love of the activity. All you have to give up is the notion that the world *must* reward you the way *you* see fit. Let the world determine its half of the trade.

IT'S UNREALISTIC TO EXPECT THAT

- Just because you like an activity, you can make a living at it.
- Just because you like somebody, they will like you back.
- Just because you worked hard at something, you *must* succeed at it.
- Just because you have many important goals, you can find the time and energy to develop all of them.
- Just because you failed at something, you are not good at it.
- Just because you're good at something, you'll be successful pursuing it.
- Just because you're the most qualified person for a job, you will get it.
- Just because you have a college degree, companies will always want to hire you.
- Just because you are talented, you won't have to market and promote yourself (like everyone else!)
- Just because you exist, the world owes you a living. It doesn't. Expect to trade your valuable time, effort, and cooperation for what you need. Moreover, expect to *compete* with others to make your living.

As suggested in Chapter 4, you must learn to limit your goals to become effective. If you expect to work at a full-time job, spend an hour or two each day with your family, write a book, practice the piano, learn French, play tournament tennis, belong to the bowling league, and do the lawn on weekends— you'll quickly burn yourself out. It *is* possible to do all these things, if you only spend a few minutes at them each day. Usually, however, it's more satisfying to prioritize the activities and pursue only the more significant ones.

ELIMINATE EXCUSES AND PROCRASTINATION

Have you noticed that some people are expert at postponing the very things they most want to do? To rationalize this, they develop a careful alibi that explains why they can't do it *right now*.

> An elderly couple went to a marriage counselor to inquire about a divorce. They were ninety-five years old and had been married for seventy years. The counselor said, "Gee, you've been married so long. Why do you want to split up now?"
>
> The couple replied, "Well, we decided we should get a divorce forty years ago. You know, though, divorce is very tough on the kids. We wanted to avoid putting this terrible burden on them. So we waited for the kids to die before we did it."

Procrastination appears to be a useless fault, but it actually has an important "secondary payoff": It lets you "win" by not losing, by not having your dreams crushed. Thus, procrastination is a means by which we avoid challenging our wishful thinking with reality.

The ways by which we can procrastinate are limited only by our imagination. People who procrastinate are always:

■ Preparing

■ Gaining necessary resources

■ Waiting for the perfect opportunity or moment

■ Practicing more

■ Waiting for permission

- Waiting until they become perfectly clear about their goals
- Waiting until the competition is not so intense
- Hesitating to take action for fear of hurting loved ones
- Waiting until they finish prior obligations

When we procrastinate, we justify our behavior with *excuses*. Excuses are sometimes valid, but often we use them to avoid the difficulty we fear facing. Excuses are white lies we tell ourselves:

- I'll do it later when I'm not so tired.
- I need to mow the lawn first.
- I can't do that until I have my college degree.
- I'll wait until the children are grown.
- I can't write that chapter until I'm inspired.
- My brother needed help this year, so I never got to it.

The ironic thing about excuses is that they are true—at one level. You probably *were* tired, you probably *did* need to mow the lawn. Although all these statements may be true, they are not the *entire* truth. The entire truth is: You were motivated to avoid the task. Excuses play upon the difference between inward intention and outward expression. They allow the partial truth to cover up the whole truth. Your underlying intention was covered up with an outwardly plausible reason.

Excuses are so ingrained that they are habitual and automatic. Yet, when they are pointed out to us, we become extremely defensive and resentful.

"Always preparing, but never doing" is a subtle form of procrastination. It carries the hidden benefit that the person can hold a goal, but never act on it, and therefore never encounter resistance in the outside world. The internal critic says, "You do not know enough, you do not have enough resources, you do not have enough ability to act yet. Practice more, get another degree, acquire more resources."

This internal critic insists on more practicing and discourages doing for real. "Doing for real" means doing in relationship with the outside world. Doing for real opens up the possibility of both liabilities and benefits. Doing for real means you are also *learning* what works. With practicing, you don't really learn, because you are doing it in a vacuum or an artificial environment.

Procrastination allows you to maintain an unrealistic estimate of your own abilities. By putting off the test in the real world, you can rationalize that you *could* succeed at a particular task *if* you were to attempt it. Since the real evidence never materializes, your opinion of your ability goes unchallenged. As long as you procrastinate, you will never be judged less than you imagine yourself. You can avoid the humiliation of doing it and not performing as well as you had expected. Thus, you avoid the possibility of failure by putting off the task indefinitely.

> ## As long as you procrastinate, you will never be judged less than you imagine yourself.

Perfectionism is often the root cause of procrastination. Everyone has a fear of failure—to some extent. For perfectionists, though, the fear of failure is especially strong. They prefer to put off doing something if there is *any* chance that they'll do less than spectacularly. Perfectionists discover that this attitude toward failure severely limits their own growth.

Perfectionists have an all-or-nothing stance in the way they look at their own performance. Either they do things perfectly—without a single slip or mistake—or the performance is completely bad, useless, and unacceptable. Because they can only be satisfied with perfection, they are continually disappointed in their imperfect, but nevertheless adequate, performances.

This all-or-nothing outlook is dangerous because it leads to discouragement. Perfectionists stop trying at the first sign of less than perfect performance. Because consummate performance requires much practice, perfectionists bail out before they give themselves a chance. They're constantly looking for situations in which they can become instant experts or prodigies without any chance of meeting criticism or failure along the way. Perfectionists would do well to meditate on the old Sufi saying, "No man attains the state of perfection until a thousand honest people have declared him a heretic."

Another source of procrastination is an inordinate sensitivity to power and authority issues. If the need to avoid being controlled dominates your psychological life, making decisions can be very difficult. Most decisions involve committing yourself to people or courses of action that *depend* on people. Once you've played your hand this way, you're no longer invulnerable from reactions by the other involved parties. They may criticize you, humiliate you, probe your weaknesses, or take delight at your very first mistake!

By procrastinating, you can avoid this situation altogether. You can pull back from the decisions, commitments, and relationships that could go awry and leave you vulnerable. No one can hurt you, discourage you, tell you "I told you so," or actively interfere with your plans. Thus uncommitted, you can pretend that you have more freedom this way. But this is a very sterile freedom. True, you avoid the possibility that your commitments can backfire and control you. However, the only option you are supporting this way is one of *escape*.

People who avoid commitment often have a childhood in which they have been unfairly manipulated or controlled. They want to prevent that situation of vulnerability again at all costs. From their point of view, having committed relationships is more a liability than an asset. The price of the relationship is acceding to the overcontrolling tendencies of the other party (the internalized parent). They fail to acknowledge that you can't accomplish very much in life all by yourself.

The best thing that can happen to this kind of person is to learn experientially that a relationship does not necessarily equate with being controlled. Therapy might be helpful in finally coming to terms with an unfortunate childhood situation. As a child, the person probably did not have any options other than to accede to the overcontrolling parent ("obey or else"). As an adult, however, a person has much more say about his or her relationships. People can negotiate, compromise, fight fairly, or hold their ground—and are not helpless to protect their own interests.

In many situations in adult life, you'll have to play by other people's rules to derive the benefits you want. If you want a college degree, a job with a particular employer, or a membership in the local country club—you'll have to abide by their rules to get the rewards. Usually, playing by other people's rules will not destroy your sense of autonomy or personhood. You can maneuver within their rules to avoid many of the negatives. Further, to some extent, you have the choice of *which* game you want to play and *with whom* you want to play it. There are great differences between the available options. The responsibility to find, discern, and choose from among them is yours.

6

DEVELOP A SUCCESS PLAN

YOU ARE A FIVE-STAR GENERAL

War is a good model for decision making. In war, other people are competing for the same things you want. Your enemies try to defeat you or undermine your purposes. To wage a war, you must strengthen your abilities to fight, to gather intelligence, and to set goals. Moreover, war forces you to recognize the limitations on your resources. Mustering allies, support, and supplies can be just as important as the fighting itself.

In a war, there are winners and losers, rewards and losses. To increase the chances of victory, generals create *plans* to achieve their goals. When it comes to your own decisions, you are the general, and it is *you* who must make the plans.

WARFARE —— DECISION MAKING

Setting of goals

Long-term strategies

Short-term tactics

Alliances

Resistance

Timing

Will power and courage

Gathering intelligence/information

Planning of campaigns

Mustering resources

Declaring one's position

Committing to a course of action

Fighting to overcome obstacles

Risk of losing

I hope my allusion to war does not offend your peace-loving sensibilities. I mention this analogy because it highlights an undeniable aspect of decision making: Implementing decisions almost always results in a certain amount of resistance from the outside world. (The exceptions are decisions of the "play it completely safe" variety, where you remain in a self-imposed cocoon.)

Understanding that this resistance is natural will help you deal better with the emotional aspects of decision making. Everyone around you will *tend* to resist your new plans or behavior. People are used to the old you, to the old plan. It's human nature to assume that you will continue to act as you have in the past. People like predictability. Change—any change—is stressful, and people find it difficult to accept.

Those who resist your decisions and plans may accuse you of being selfish or irresponsible. Their accusations may or may not be true. It's up to *you* to determine where the exact boundary between selfishness and justifiable self-interest lies. Setting these boundaries is claiming responsibility for the direction of your own life.

Implementing decisions almost always results in resistance from the outside world.

A PLAN CONNECTS HERE-NOW
WITH THERE-THEN

Planning simulates the flow of future events. It allows you to try out actions on paper (or in your head) without committing yourself to acting in the real world. By predicting the consequences of the planned actions, you can compare the soundness of various courses of action and select the most promising.

A plan looks at *future* actions, actions that will lead to your goals. If none of your alternatives steers you to where you want to go, you need to restate your decision. There are two ways that you can connect here-now with a future there-then. With *forward chaining*, you ask of each alternative, "Where does this lead and do I want that new situation?" In a logical sense, you're starting with your present situation and moving forward on a path to your eventual goal. The second method is *backward chaining*, where you state the end point or goal and try to find the intermediate steps that can get you there. With backward chaining, you first ask what step immediately preceding the goal is necessary to reach the goal. Then you ask what step immediately preceding that will bring you there. And so on, until you have "backed" your way down to your present position.

A plan reduces anxiety by focusing your energies and keeping you on track. By emphasizing actions rather than thoughts, a plan allows you to step, little by little, toward your goals. Actions yield much more information and useful results than contemplation and worry. Making a plan shows that you take the prospective venture seriously. A plan reduces the tendency to daydream about your goals, and instead, urges you to take concrete actions.

Tom came to me with an expression of agony on his face. He said, "I'm sick of the company I work for. I want out. I want to become a consultant right away and take my leave of nagging bosses and impossible demands."

I replied, "Becoming a consultant sounds great to me, but *how* are you going to do it?"

Tom paused for a second and then offered, "First I'll tell those bastards to go to hell. Then I'll rent an office downtown and inform all my friends about my consulting services."

"Whoa," I said, "To start, let's take an inventory of your resources and situation." (A quick assessment revealed that Tom was long on anger but short on cash and surefire business contacts.)

Tom said, "Okay, so I don't tell them off. What should I do instead?"

I told him, "What you need is a *plan.* You need to develop a set of tasks and a timetable that will allow you to decide a year from now whether consulting is for you. You have very little cash and have never consulted before, so intermediate goals should be established before you leap in with both feet."

"Get your first consulting contract on a moonlighting basis while you are with your present employer."

"Over the next year, build up your client list and cash position. At the end of the year, you'll have both the money and the experience to make a better decision. In particular, you will know the market demand for your services and how much you like consulting."

"If, at the end of this year, consulting doesn't work out, you have a fall-back position at your present company, which may have changed for the better in the meantime. Or you may find an attractive job at one of the companies you have moonlighted for."

Tom looked disappointed. He asked, "Isn't there any way I can tell those bastards to go to hell?"

I said, "No, but if you're looking for a coping technique, I have just the thing. The next time someone slights you in a company meeting, take a chocolate cream pie and push it in their face."

Tom exclaimed, "Are you crazy? I can't do that!"

"I know, Tom. But the *thought* of doing it will help you hang in there for another year."

Planning is one way to make sure you *don't leave things to chance*. For example, suppose you are on a diet. If you forget to plan for meals while traveling, you're much more likely to end up eating high-calorie food at a restaurant. Planning in this situation would be finding the locations of diet-oriented restaurants ahead of time or bringing your own special meals with you.

PLANNING IN A NUTSHELL

1. Formulate your goal in clear terms.

2. Inventory present resources and situation.

3. Describe resources needed to achieve goal.

4. Propose a sequence of intermediate steps.

5. Examine the feasibility of the plan.

6. Make the plan flexible.

7. Use time management to implement the plan.

Another example of planning is in giving a speech. Beginning speech makers are terrified of the possibility that someone will ask a question that they can't handle. Experienced presenters, on the other hand, don't leave such things to chance. They prepare in advance for likely questions and have extra materials on hand, should they be required.

Not leaving things to chance means taking positive actions that minimize the possibility of negative situations later on. This insurance policy approach can be overdone, but in critical situations, the extra effort and expense are usually worth it. A final example: A couple wants an outdoor wedding. They are concerned that if it rains, the event will be ruined. One way to plan for this is to arrange for a canopy large enough to handle the wedding party. Rain or shine, this special event will proceed smoothly.

A PLAN IS RATIONAL AND REALISTIC

The desire for your goal need not be rational, but the plan itself *must* be rational. It must be based on how the world actually works. That is, you can use your imagination to find the goal, but a plan uses knowledge of the world "as it is." Because a decision is a commitment to a plan of action, if it doesn't take these significant factors into account, it will fail. "How things work" is not luxury knowledge but knowledge essential to success.

Do your planning while dispassionate. When planning, physically remove yourself from any negative situations in which you may be involved. Arrange a quiet time and place. Getting away from your usual environment often helps. Indeed, many large corporations do their planning off-site. Constant interruption at the office interferes with the concentration that good planning requires.

When you are making an important decision in one area of your life, try to keep the other areas as steady as possible. Trying to decide on two or three major areas at once can overload your emotional capacity to deal with uncertainty and anxiety. When approaching a decision, try to let your psychic momentum in positive areas of your life carry you through the tough spots.

"How things work" is not luxury knowledge but knowledge essential to success.

The next section will help you examine the feasibility of your plan. It will make it easier for you to judge whether your plan brings you to the goal (or even one step closer).

A PLAN MAKES EXPLICIT THE RESOURCES NEEDED AND THE TIMETABLE FOR ACTION

Planning is not just "thinking" about the actions you intend to take in the future. *Planning makes things concrete.* It sketches sufficient detail to allow you to carry out a coherent course of action. It integrates the individual tasks leading up to the desired result. There are five essential points in judging the quality of a plan.

A good plan is *specific*. It provides milestones of significant events so that you can monitor your progress.

A good plan is *explicit*. It spells out the timetable and the needed resources. It declares your actions in clear, straightforward terms. It provides concrete measures to monitor your progress. One way to assure that your plan is explicit is to put it in writing (unless, of course, you're planning a Watergate break-in or a bank robbery!).

Written plans serve two important functions. First, they allow you to verify whether you've considered the major issues. Second, they are records of your decision-making process. These prove invaluable at a later date in refreshing your memory, at improving the process, and at checking the accuracy of your judgment: Did you gauge other people correctly? Were you on target in estimating the resources needed? Did you foresee significant changes in the environment? Were you able to spot a trend before it "burst" upon the scene? Were you biased against certain options that could have helped you? Did you trust your own perceptions or listen more to people who claimed to know better than you? Did you define the issues correctly in the first place?

A good plan is *efficient*. It avoids an excess of wasted footsteps. Although some waste is inevitable in any series of actions, a plan tends to minimize the amount. Good plans prevent aimless drifting and ineffective measures.

> A man came into a cocktail lounge and ordered a martini. While he was sipping his drink, he took out a small jar from his coat pocket. He picked the olive out of the martini and put it in the jar. A few minutes later, he ordered another martini and did the same thing. After an hour, when the man was full of martinis and the jar was full of olives, he staggered out.
>
> "Wow," said a customer, "I've never seen anything as bizarre as that."
>
> "What's so weird about it?" the bartender replied. "His wife sent him out for a jar of olives."

A good plan *reflects a set of priorities* that allows you to focus your energies in useful directions. Without such priorities, you would not know which tasks to do first. Italian economist Vilfredo Pareto offered some insight on how to examine priorities. About 100 years ago, he proposed his *80/20 rule*. It says that in most human endeavors, 80 percent of the successful results can be attributed to only 20 percent of the causes. For example, in a business 80 percent of the sales typically comes from only 20 percent of the customers. And at work, 80 percent of the useful results typically comes from only 20 percent of the effort. Pareto's rule holds profound advice for planners: Look for areas that have high payoff and concentrate on them *first*.

A good plan *uses time management.* It helps you "chunk out" the day, so that your activities reflect the plan you have set for yourself. Without time management, you may experience the frustrating sense that "your life is running you." With careful time management, however, you can balance many areas in your life without undue stress. You can reward yourself at the end of the day for work well done.

Time management helps you avoid time-gobblers like the telephone, TV, window shopping, junk mail, and so on. It helps you use time more efficiently by combining tasks. For example, you can combine separate shopping trips into a single trip that requires fewer miles driven and less total time. You can make meal preparation more efficient by cooking extra meat or chicken and freezing the leftovers for quick meals. You can make your dining-out business luncheons more efficient by meeting with more than one friend at a time.

Finally, time management urges you to *choose your toys carefully.* Boats, cars, power tools, swimming pools, recreational vehicles, sewing machines, vacation homes, lawn mowers, stereos, and computers are wonderful. Yet, the more of these toys you own, the more time you spend maintaining them (or paying someone else to). There is much merit to Thoreau's maxim, "Simplify, simplify."

People who have a psychological resistance to time management pooh-pooh it. They insist that they want to "let things happen more naturally." Yet, these are the very same people who never accomplish their goals! They don't take themselves seriously enough to risk scheduling and organizing their day-to-day efforts. The prize for this self-defeating attitude is that they can never disappoint themselves, because they have never stated their goal in a way that can be measured.

Learning how to handle interruptions is one of the most important talents a decision maker can acquire. At first, you may not feel that you're in a position to put others off. ("How can I tell my boss that I'm not going to drop everything and help him with his panic fire drill?") But I guarantee you, if you don't start making a stand somewhere, people will *learn* that you are a pushover, that it's okay to interrupt you when you have important things to do.

Naturally, some interruptions *are* unavoidable. The secret in minimizing them is to let others know that you value your time and that there are situations in which you *justifiably* cannot respond immediately to their requests. "Justifiably" means that you must be prepared to explain *why* you are putting off the interruption and why it is *reasonable* to do so. It's like being your own lawyer: Plead your case and hold firm to your ground.

Train people to respect your time, energy, and money. Some people may take your good will for granted. They may assume that you will always be there to bail them out because you did it before. Training others requires that you have sufficient self-esteem to demand that they not ignore your best interests. Your ability to rebuff interruptions will improve with practice. If you feel uncomfortable handling interruptions, taking a course in self-assertiveness may prove valuable.

> ## You must *train* certain people to respect your time, energy, and money.

SOME TIME-HONORED WAYS
TO HANDLE AN INTERRUPTION

- Refuse it. (Simply say "No.")

- Postpone your response. ("I can't do it now, but maybe tomorrow.")

- Negotiate for mutual benefit. ("I'll help you only if ———."
  Fill in conditions that provide you a compensating benefit.)

- Delegate it. ("I can't do this; it's John's problem.")

- Ignore it.

- Limit it. ("You can have five minutes of my time.")

■ Interrupt the interrupter. ("By the way, before I can listen
to your problem, you promised me . . . .")

■ Arrange to be called away on an even higher priority
("the doctor's beeper gambit").

■ Set up a buffer between yourself and the interruption.
Get a secretary or answering machine. Sometimes the
buffer is spatial: If you have trouble concentrating on
your work, find another work space that's more conducive
to it.

■ Limit your commitments. Do not be sweet-talked into tasks
that sap your time, energy, and resources.

MAKE YOUR PLAN FLEXIBLE

A good plan anticipates major problems and finds ways to
address them. Professional decision makers call this *contingency*
planning. The steps are simple:

1. Define what would constitute a major threat or problem.

2. List the additional resources, effort, or strategies that would be
required to overcome the problem.

3. Determine if these responses allow you to adapt to the contingencies while continuing the pursuit of your goal.

4. List the alternate paths that could be pursued.

5. Do a worst case analysis: Could you handle the worst case if it
happened?

A flexible plan offers many ways to accomplish the goal.
It considers additional strategies to reach the goal when outside
events change the premises upon which the decision was based.
The key to flexibility is *adapting* to changes, finding ways to
respond without giving up the goal. A flexible plan does not
fall apart when minor crises strike. Instead, it draws on your
internal resources, strength, and willingness to deviate from the
charted course and navigate around obstacles.

The opposite of flexibility is rigidity, sticking to a single
strategy, even when it's not working. This brings us to a subtle
point in decision making. There is a difference between *flexibility*
and *lack of perseverance*. Flexibility is a virtue. Lack of perse-

verance, on the other hand, is a fault. It means abandoning valid strategies simply because you lacked the guts to hang in there for a brief spell of rough weather. Because very few strategies give instantaneous results, you need staying power. Only after you have given a particular strategy a *real* chance should you move on to another.

The issue of specialization is relevant here. Specializing has benefits in many situations. When you concentrate in a single area, you become more cost-effective, efficient, and knowledgeable (within that field). Yet, specializing makes you less flexible. It becomes more difficult to adapt. Therefore, if your plan involves specializing, you should also consider ways to widen your activities simultaneously. If you must specialize in your job, for example, devote a small amount of time to developing general skills. It's okay to spend some of your time in a narrow area; just don't lock yourself into it! Similarly, if your social contexts are very limited, join an athletic group, social club, or church to expose yourself to new people, ideas, and activities.

Here is an interesting paradox: A plan may be flexible, while the individual who makes the plan may be inflexible. The result is usually a rigid response. That is, rigid personality overpowers flexible intention. To become flexible, you must *practice* being flexible. You must practice reacting in a variety of modes other than the habitual or planned ones. If the environment does not provide the occasion to exercise your flexibility as a natural response, then you must create your own "flexibility drills." Flexibility is a learned talent.

Flexible decision makers avoid—by conscientious effort—limiting their own horizons by falling into habitual repetition. They remain flexible by intentionally introducing a certain amount of change in their life, constantly challenging themselves. Becoming flexible is a kind of investment in themselves.

Flexibility is a learned talent.

Flexibility is a reflection of our attitude toward change. The rigid person dislikes change so much that they remain stagnant. When significant events appear on the horizon, they rationalize away the obvious need to consider their options and react accordingly. Their reluctance to practice change under average conditions leads to a total inability to change when under pressure. Their emotional resources are overwhelmed when they are faced with an urgent predicament. The flexible person, on the other hand, is sensitive to important outside events. They are willing and able to risk and experiment when the situation calls for it.

Although I've said a mouthful about plans here, I hope I have not given the impression that they need to be complex. Certainly, many things must be considered. But simple plans are often the best, especially when you are testing them for feasibility.

Complex plans rarely work the way they are designed. There are too many things that can go wrong at once. It's easier in most situations to devise a simple plan and then build on it as you go along. Rely on your resourcefulness to improvise. When dealing with a complex situation, however, one useful principle is to create a *general* strategy. This states the goal in a general way, but leaves open those major items that cannot be resolved at the moment. The tactics used at any one time to carry out the decision are then measured against the general goal.

HOW TO BECOME A FLEXIBLE PLANNER

- Monitor the environment for events and trends that affect you.

- Structure the plan incrementally. It's easier to change a plan if you have broken it down into a number of parts that can be individually modified.

- Observe whether the plan is working. Determine the ways in which it is not working and restructure those components, being careful to salvage, if possible, those components that do work.

- Practice flexibility in situations where the stakes are low.

7

SEIZE OPPORTUNITIES

TWO WAYS OF ACHIEVING YOUR GOALS: STRATEGIES AND TACTICS

In the last chapter, we discussed planning as a means of developing long-range strategies to achieve your goals. These long-range strategies are *goal driven*. They depend mostly on thoughtful elaboration of your goals and how you intend to achieve them in a general sense.

There's another way of achieving your goals. It complements long-range planning, but does not replace it. This second way is to take advantage of opportunities as they present themselves. In warfare, this is called the art of tactics. Tactics are *opportunity driven*. They depend more on external events than on your own planning. With tactics, you hitch yourself to a rising star or make an advantageous trade in order to gain a better strategic position.

Developing good strategies comes first. Strategies tell you the general direction you're going in. Yet, because strategies look at the big picture, they cannot account for unplanned situations encountered along the way that make your progress faster or easier. Tactics use these opportunities to enhance and supplement strategy.

Correct use of tactics involves a keen sense of judging external situations. Be it in war, business, romance, or employment, the tactician looks for moves that will secure personal advantage or that lead one step closer to the accomplishment of overall purposes. Tactical moves have long been categorized in books on warfare and negotiation. Some of the most popular ones are:

- Get your foot in the door (set a precedent)
- Surprise the opponent
- Use a decoy (disguise your motives or create a diversion)
- Form alliances with the powerful
- Blackmail, bribery, flattery
- Catch others in their moment of need (find desperate buyers/sellers)
- Bait and switch
- Divide and conquer (set two powerful enemies against each other)
- Feign weakness, insolvency, or incompetence to gain advantage

Tactics can be combined to great effect. Here is how one decision maker used the tactic of delaying his reactions and followed it with the tactic of surprise:

> A truck driver pulled off Route 1 and went into a roadside diner to have lunch. He asked the waitress to bring him a burger, some fries, and a cup of coffee. As the waitress set his lunch before him, three tough motorcyclists wearing leather jackets and chains sat down beside him at the counter. One snatched the burger out of his hand and ate it. Another grabbed his coffee and guzzled it down. The third stuck two fries up his own nostrils with a sneering gesture and then mashed the rest of the fries on the plate.

The truck driver said nothing. He got up, paid the cashier for lunch, and walked out. The three toughs turned to the cashier, and one said, "Not much of a man, is he?"

"He's not much of a driver, either," replied the cashier. "He just ran his truck over three motorcycles."

As useful as tactics are, it's dangerous to depend too heavily on them. *Opportunists* are people who forsake all long-term planning for short-term advantage. They lose focus of the big picture and make short-term moves that ignore or contradict their eventual goals. They become so enamored of tactics that they elevate this kind of bargain hunting to a goal, even when they don't need the item in question.

One secret of effective decision making is, therefore, balance strategy and tactics. The two activities are not mutually exclusive. You should *always* have (and be improving) a long-range strategy. You should *always* be aware of the kinds of opportunities that will benefit your position. A good decision maker—as well as a good warrior—uses both strategies and tactics.

Balance strategy and tactics!

Planning is a strategic activity that works best in an uncrowded world. As a field becomes more and more crowded, planning becomes increasingly difficult. You can gain an appreciation for this from the figure "Two Ways of Reaching Your Goal." It shows a person trying to cross a reception room in two different situations. When the room is empty, the person can simply plot a course ("plan") and go directly to the goal. When the room is full of people, this linear plan will not work without collisions. For the crowded condition, seeking opportunities ("tactics") becomes increasingly attractive as a means of getting to the goal. One such opportunity might be to wait for a food tray to be wheeled across the room. You could then follow in its wake with relatively little effort.

Putting this principle in practical terms: In an uncrowded field, success depends on what *you* do; in a crowded field, it depends on how you take advantage of what *others* do.

WAYS OF EVALUATING OPPORTUNITIES: OPTIMIZING, SATISFICING, AND DISOWNING

An opportunity is an external situation that offers us a time-limited choice. If we wait too long, like Immanuel Kant and the neighbor's daughter in Chapter 2, we may find that the choice is no longer available.

Opportunities are abundant. Whether or not we're aware of it, opportunities of various sorts constantly appear to each and every one of us. In decision making, therefore, it is useful to know: How do I recognize an opportunity? What kind of opportunities are of interest to me? How do I evaluate them?

The optimizing approach to evaluating opportunities says that the answer is to consider *all* possible choices at any moment, and then choose the best option. It presumes that you have the time and energy to assemble a large number of viable options from which to choose. Optimizing is a very useful technique in business, where it is important to squeeze the last dollar of profit from an existing system. By selecting the supplier with the lowest cost, selecting the retail outlets with the greatest profit margin, refining the operation of the distribution network, and choosing the most advantageous advertising deals, the business can be fine-tuned to optimal profitability.

You can also use optimization in purchasing a new car. If you have the inclination, time, and energy, you could go to *all* the dealers' showrooms in your area. You could then compare *all* the different models for features, performance, reliability, appearance, and price. The one that best suits your criteria is the optimal choice.

Optimization is a great way to evaluate opportunities if:

■ You have many alternatives available.

■ All these alternatives are open to you at the same time.

■ You have the time and energy to compare and evaluate them all.

The problem is, these conditions are often not satisfied in many decision situations. In practice, most decisions are based on the *replacement model*. This says that at a single moment in time, we must evaluate our present situation and decide whether or not to replace it with another opportunity that becomes available.

TWO WAYS OF REACHING YOUR GOAL

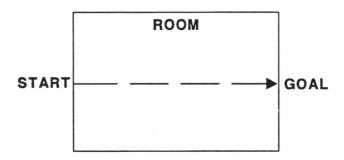

PLANNING WORKS BEST IN AN UNCROWDED WORLD.
When the room is empty, you can go directly to
the other side.

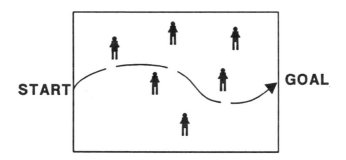

OPPORTUNITY WORKS BEST IN A CROWDED WORLD.
When the room is full, you need more effort to reach
the goal. Or you could look for an opportunity (e.g.,
wait for a food tray to be wheeled across the room
and travel in its wake)

For example, Suzy has been dating Johnny for two years. He is her next-door neighbor, and it was convenient to start a romance with him. It was also safe, because they already knew each other well. Nevertheless, Suzy is not entirely satisfied with their relationship. In the past two years, she has discovered that Johnny has completely different values about marriage and family. Suzy meets someone new who is more interesting and better suited to her. She asks herself, "Should I drop Johnny and start dating this new person?"

In this choice, Suzy is not trying to optimize. She could have done this, to some extent, by playing the field, which would greatly widen the options available to her. Instead, she did what is practical and acceptable in many life situations. She posed the decision in terms of the replacement model: Keep Johnny or date Mr. New? Suzy knows the pros and cons of dating Johnny, but must guess about the outcome if she dates Mr. New. Changing from her present situation involves this element of uncertainty and risk.

The replacement model almost always presents the decision maker with an uneven set of data. Yet, it's more commonly used than optimizing because the time and energy to explore all other opportunities may not be available. Choosing with the replacement model can be very effective, though, if you have developed the experience that leads to sound judgment.

Economist Herbert Simon developed the concept of *satisficing* to explain why the replacement model is so useful in everyday life. Satisficing helps you decide, "When is 'good' good enough?"

Simon maintains that satisficing is valuable because it acknowledges the *principle of bounded rationality*. This principle says that we, as humans, possess only a limited ability to process all the information that might be needed to make a complex decision. It is human nature to simplify problems so as to be able to arrive at decisions at all. If we tried to consider complex problems in a precise way, to optimize and find the very best solution, we would overtax the capability of our minds. So we settle for a reasonable or "good enough" solution that solves the problem adequately.

When you're searching for a job, for example, it's not practical to hold out for the optimal situation. You may have a very long wait! After years of seeking, you may discover that the perfect job does not exist as a ready-made thing. For most of us, the pressure of having to earn a living demands some form of compromise.

The satisficing approach is to select options that meet minimal, yet important, criteria for salary, work content, and working conditions. If the opportunities meeting these criteria are few and far between (that is, if a dozen different employers are not beating your door down!), the first one that satisfies your minimum criteria is chosen. Once this commitment has been made, the search ends. If a subsequent job offer appears, most people resist the impulse to "incrementally optimize." That is, they do not accept later offers with only *slightly* greater benefits. A 1 percent salary increase would not be sufficient incentive to leave a situation that is otherwise acceptable.

After you have made a satisficing decision, elements of risk and uncertainty remain, even if things go well initially. This is not cause for alarm or skepticism, though. The conclusion to be drawn from it is that even in acceptable situations, you should still be aware of your other options. Especially with regard to employment issues, continually monitor and improve your marketability by increasing your competence and circle of contacts. The confidence that you are competent and marketable reduces the fear of making mistakes in job transitions.

Sometimes, you may not be able to find *any* alternative that meets your minimum criteria. In such cases, it's useful to consider the *one step closer* criterion. Ask yourself, "Which remaining alternatives bring me one step closer to what I ultimately want?"

To evaluate an opportunity, ask yourself:

- Is it consistent with my long-range plans?
- Is it better than my present situation?
- Should I take up this opportunity or wait for a more suitable one?
- What are the risks presented by this opportunity? Can I tolerate them?
- Does accepting this opportunity set any significant precedents? Are they consistent with my values?

■ When is "good" good enough? When should I stop actively looking for further opportunities and work at enjoying or improving my present options?

The *one step closer* criterion is an indirect method. It's an effective compromise when you are stuck, but must nevertheless get on with things. It should be made with the understanding that you'll take further action when better opportunities appear.

Disowning is the third broad method of evaluating opportunities. It means that you choose the first opportunity that comes along, regardless of whether it meets any of your criteria. Disowning mirrors the attitude that you don't *care* what happens in your own life, that all options are the same.

Disowning was romanticized by French writers like Sartre and Camus, who suffered through France's humiliation in World War II. Their writing reflected the wave of alienation and frustration that swept through their country after the fall. Indeed, at that time, most Frenchmen *were* powerless to affect the events in their life. No matter what they did, they were swept along by forces much stronger than themselves. For our times, though, disowning has no redeeming quality or poetic merit. It's simply a pathetic way to make choices.

THE FLEA MARKET MODEL

I have often experienced flea market shopping as an exercise in practical decision making. At the flea market, I'm surrounded with an abundance of objects for sale. In making purchases, I not only have to recognize the things that I'm interested in, but I also have to figure out whether I'm willing to pay the price. (It's not quite that simple because the price is often negotiated.)

Since I have only a limited amount of money, I must choose wisely. Flea market shopping is a safe way to learn to say "no" to those things that either do not fit my needs or whose price is higher than I'm willing to pay, no matter how attractive the item may be. In short, flea market shopping helps me become a better and more confident trader. It teaches me how to make trades that are to my benefit. It provides practice in declining deals that—for any reason—do not suit me.

Flea market shopping is a miniature Gestalt[1] exercise on "Who I am" and "Who I am not." It teaches you how to extract the things you want from the environment in a safe and painless way.

One idea I gained from flea marketing applies to life in general: To make wise purchases (decisions), you really have to understand what's out there and what the going prices are. In Gestalt terminology, you have to be *involved in the game.*

When something nice arrives at a dealer's table, you can be sure it will be snapped up in short order. Thus, you must be prepared for quick action when good opportunities present themselves. You must already have well-developed tastes (self-knowledge) to know if you're interested in the item. You must already have a knowledge of the market to know what's available and whether a similar opportunity is likely to occur soon again. And you must already have a sense of market values to know whether you are getting a good deal.

> ## To make wise decisions, you must be *involved* in the game.

Often, you must decide right on the spot whether to buy it, without comparison shopping the other vendors. Unless you are wealthy enough to buy everything you see, you must choose based on an incomplete search.

These flea market maxims apply to developing judgment in general: To make good evaluations of opportunities as they arise, you must create a background of experience in similar

---

[1] Gestalt therapy was developed by psychoanalyst Fritz Perls in the 1940s. It emphasizes improving awareness of self (inner world) and environment (outer world) in the "here and now." Gestalt therapy does this by teaching individuals how to overcome "obsessive remembering of the past" and "anxious anticipation of the future." See *The Gestalt Approach* (1973) by Fritz Perls for a lucid exposition, especially as it applies to the decision-related issues of identity, defining needs, and contacting the environment to satisfy needs.

situations or use other people's advice, based on their experience of similar situations. To choose well requires that you already have a good idea of what is acceptable and how that alternative suits you. When opportunities present themselves, you will often have little time to deliberate, experiment, or negotiate extensively. These internal standards allow you to judge the adequacy of opportunities as they arrive at random times.

WHEN TO SEEK OUT OPPORTUNITIES

Under what circumstances should you be seeking opportunities in contrast to implementing long-range planning? And how do you define the need to seek out opportunities?

Opportunities offer ways to fulfill *needs*. If your needs are more or less satisfied, you won't be interested in seeking out opportunities. You can just maintain a steady course with your plan. If you are unaware of your needs, you won't be able to recognize worthwhile opportunities, even if they are staring you in the face!

Once unsatisfied needs become apparent, you'll be open to opportunities that could fulfill them. If you're not getting exposure to the kind of opportunities you find useful, you must change your methods, attitudes, or the circles you travel in. If opportunities don't find you, you must find them. Join new groups, meet new people, do new things—until you start getting the kind of results you want. It takes patience and courage to experiment with unfamiliar territory, but the results are invariably productive.

Opportunities are far more abundant than we are willing to admit. What is rare is the ability to recognize them. If you don't *already* have a mental image of the situations you desire, certain opportunities will remain invisible to you. Sometimes, though, even a change in attitude is enough to make previously invisible opportunities visible.

If opportunities don't find you, you must find them.

Exploring new opportunities does not mean that you must abandon your old group of friends. You merely have to widen your circle of exposure. The key concept is that opportunities exist apart from you. They are out there in the environment, in the world that surrounds you. Your job is to find them and see if they provide good matches for your purposes. From this point of view, creating opportunities is a misnomer. Instead of inventing them out of thin air, we arrive at new opportunities most often by acknowledging or restructuring opportunities that already exist.

If, after much searching, you discover that the wanted opportunities do *not* exist, do not be discouraged: You have gained some very valuable information. You have learned that you must modify your expectations about the kinds of opportunities available or implement your own long-range plan without using tactics ("slogging through it").

Seeking out opportunities soaks up emotional energies. In reaching out to the environment in this way, you're putting yourself on the line. Negotiating with others to get the things you need can be frustrating and disheartening. Affirmations may help you maintain your self-esteem in this process. See Chapter 11 for an explanation of why such affirmations are essential.

RULES OF THUMB

If you had to consider fully every opportunity that presented itself, you'd quickly run out of time and energy. Rules of thumb (heuristics) save you time and mental effort in these everyday decisions. They conserve your effort and judgment for the decisions that really matter.

Heuristics reduce the task of making a complex judgment into a simple yes/no operation. Because they simplify, they carry the danger of sometimes being inappropriate. Rules of thumb are really *guesses* based on the most common way that the problem has been solved before. Rules of thumb should be questioned when the particular problem differs from the rule in an essential way or is too important to be quickly categorized and handled. Rejecting a rule-of-thumb approach means that you accept the problem as worthy of consideration from first principles. It means that you intend to commit the time and energy to search for a solution method and criteria.

Heuristics are particularly effective in two decision-making situations: evaluating opportunities and handling crises. Because crises will be discussed in Chapter 10, only opportunities are considered here.

The following list of decision heuristics presents some common rules of thumb. "Divide and conquer," for example, refers to the strategy of breaking a problem into subproblems that are more tractable. "Don't cut off your nose to spite your face" suggests that you should not sacrifice a greater goal to satisfy a lesser one. "There are no free lunches" warns you to search for hidden motives if a deal seems too good to be true. "Oil the squeaky wheel first" instructs you to pay attention to the most critical items first.

DECISION HEURISTICS

Heuristics are *rules of thumb* that reduce a complex decision into a simple yes or no. They save you time for solving your *important* problems. Here are some examples:

1. Divide and conquer.

2. A stitch in time saves nine.

3. Oil the squeaky wheel first.

4. There are no free lunches.

5. If it worked last time, try it again.

6. Don't cut off your nose to spite your face.

7. If you can't stand the heat, get out of the kitchen.

8. If it works for everybody else, it will probably work for you.

9. The more complex the decision, the more likely nothing will ever be done.

10. As a market becomes more competitive, maintaining a steady position requires increased promotional effort.

11. You should take one minute to decide on a lunch menu, one day on buying a car, one week on a job, one year on switching careers or spouses.

12. Eighty percent of all advice you receive will be wrong, misdirected, biased, inapplicable, or otherwise unusable.

13. A new business venture is unlikely to succeed if you can't express its basic operation in a single sentence.

14. A guarantee or promise made by somebody unable to back it up is worthless.

THE TIMING OF DECISIONS

Alternatives are not always simultaneous; sometimes they arrive at different times. This fact has profound implications for how we evaluate opportunities.

To try to create the situation of many alternatives existing at one moment in time—so as to satisfy the "requirements" of an optimum decision model—is to deceive oneself. The winner in a relative-ranking contest may satisfy the methodology, but might still be totally inadequate in terms of personal standards. The best policy may be to wait for new opportunities as they arise or to invest the time and energy to seek out new opportunities.

Therefore, the time frame of decision is a key factor in the specification of the decision problem. Sometimes, there may be no choice but to pick from only those alternatives that exist at that moment. In a squeeze, you pick the best among the available alternatives, even if it does not meet your standards. You are buying time to find a new opportunity that *is* acceptable. This is one way of defining survival: You tolerate not having a full range of choice today, in the hope that the available choices will be better tomorrow.

> **SURVIVAL: Tolerating the scarcity of choices today, in the hope that the choices available tomorrow will be better.**

A survival tactic is a balancing act: How much of today will you sacrifice to purchase the chance for a better tomorrow? On the one hand, it's foolish to forsake the present *totally* to improve the future. On the other hand, short-term gratifications often undermine long-term well-being. Understanding the relation between cause and effect in our actions helps develop the emotional maturity to bear some postponement. A sense of psychological security allows us to accept the risk inherent in any postponing strategy: that tomorrow may never come.

If you must make a decision in a rush, ask yourself:

- *When* does this decision need to be made?
- *Why* does it need to be made at that time? Can it be delayed?
- *What* is the penalty for delaying it? What happens if I do nothing? If I delay, can changes occurring in the meantime affect the outcome?
- *When* will the proposed alternatives be accomplished? How long does it take for a positive result to appear?
- *How* does a positive result fit into the larger plan? How does a negative result influence the larger plan?

In summary, seizing opportunities is one way you can cut big decisions down to size. Opportunities allow you to take giant strides forward in reaching your goals. To realize opportunities to the fullest, learn how to become "part of the game": Know your market, make good contacts, understand your needs, become a good trader, and be willing to pay the price.

Opportunities complement planning. Both get you to the goal, and both are usually required at one time or another. If you have made little progress in implementing a decision through planning, maybe you should be seeking opportunities. Once you develop a general idea of the kinds of opportunities that would be appropriate, find them. To avoid turning the search into an all-consuming project, use rules of thumb to sift out the good opportunities from the bad.

8

GAIN SUPPORT FOR
YOUR DECISIONS

INCLUDE SIGNIFICANT OTHERS
IN YOUR DECISION

People who love you are interested in seeing you win. Each one—in his or her own way, and to varying degrees—will support you in your decision. Some friends may offer positive vibes to your proposed plans. A few may be able to suggest contacts that will help you achieve your ends. Others may be in a position to help you out financially. Yet others may listen empathetically. (Wow!)

Unjustified compliments and unconditional praise are not really support. "Attaboys" and backslapping undermine your real confidence and self-esteem. They foster the notion that everything you do is wonderful and can't be otherwise. Useful support acknowledges the situation at hand: If you did a good job, it congratulates. If you missed the mark, it compassionately asks how you could come closer to the target. Good support *listens* and *appreciates*, but does not inflate your ego with undeserved praise.

Gaining emotional, social, and financial support is essential for the eventual success of your decisions. To do this, you must give serious consideration to who will have your best interests at heart and who will be able to be supportive. Sometimes, the very people from whom you most desire support are the least able to give it. They may be indifferent, threatened, angry, envious, or too wrapped up in their own problems. They may be so stuck in their own ways of thinking and feeling that they cannot put themselves in your shoes. Their advice may address your problem, but it will be based on *their* values.

There's no way to judge whether a person can be supportive to you without going through some of the first steps. Unless all your friends are mind readers who can guess your needs without your having to state them, you must summon the courage to *ask* for support. From their responses, you can gauge whether you want to continue pursuing their support or move on to another person who may be more able to help.

In your discussions, be sensitive to the *rapport* you establish with the other person. Are you able to talk to them frankly? Do they really listen, or are they only waiting for you to stop talking, so that they can preach their philosophy of life to you? Are they judgmental of your values or life-style? Do you trust them to respect your interests and confidentiality? Are they subtly pushing you away? Do they understand the nature of your situation and decision?

One of the best ways to gain support for your project is to ask others to help you with it. Learn whom you can trust for assistance and guidance. Many people are flattered that you think highly enough of them to ask their advice. Beyond this, they're often willing to help you with your decision in material ways. Most people feel good when they are able to lend an occasional helping hand to a friend or neighbor.

**Good support *listens* and *appreciates*,
but does not inflate your ego with
undeserved praise.**

Enlisting the help of others is essential when you are faced with a decision that involves areas that are outside the scope of your knowledge or experience. It's easier to hire a plumber or electrician or psychologist than to try to learn these fields quickly by yourself so that you can complete a particular project. This assumes, of course, that you have something to offer in trade (that is, usually, that you can afford to pay them).

There are five ways in which you can go astray in getting support:

1. *Trying to do it all yourself.* It's often tempting to undertake a project all by yourself. No one will be in a position to stop you, and you can claim 100 percent of the credit if the venture succeeds. Yet, this can be an inefficient way to do things. Certain areas of the project may be difficult for you but easy for another person. Recognize such areas and enlist that person's support, offering in return things that are easy for you.

2. *Asking others to take your risks for you* (or tell you how *you* feel). In certain situations, asking others for help can make things worse. Consider, for example, Longfellow's narrative poem, "The Courtship of Miles Standish." The powerful captain of the Plymouth settlement, Miles Standish, makes a crucial error in judgment. He asks his young friend, John Alden, to court Priscilla on his behalf. Despite John's sincerity in presenting Standish's pleas, Priscilla prefers John as a husband. ("Why don't you speak for yourself, John?") Miles avoided the possibility of rejection this way, but also lost the fair maiden.

3. *Expecting others to do all the work for you.* Some people overdo the idea of support and run around gathering a large entourage of well-wishers, contacts, and "I'll help you whenever you need it" buddies. They hope that by assembling a critical mass of such support, their goal will spontaneously materialize, just as a fission reaction occurs by bringing together a critical mass of uranium. All the supporters will pour their energies into the project, and the coach can just lie back and watch. No effort, no risk, just an occasional "Rally round the flag!" to the team. It just doesn't work this way. Support will help you come closer to your goals, but you are going to have to invest the lion's share of the energy and commitment, as well as assume the major part of the risk and liability.

People who spend *all* their effort assembling a team are frequently unsuccessful. They create an enormous flurry of promotion, arrange partnerships, and pose much "Have I got a deal for you" talk—but generate very few results. Promotion, by itself, is not sufficient to implement a decision. All the gathering of support and resources is an excuse to avoid certain kinds of effort on their own behalf.

4. *Going to people who don't care.* Believe it or not, some decision makers seek support from people who cannot or will not give it. They may ask five or ten times—in slightly different ways, of course—and still, they keep on trying. Such behavior is masochism, not persistence. Groveling in front of others destroys self-esteem. Seek support elsewhere if you cannot get it from the people you *hoped* might provide it.

5. *Wanting the other party to be supportive in every respect.* Psychologists call this the search for the mythical idealized parent. When you were an infant, your parents did, in fact, support you in every respect. They took care of your every need. As an adult, it's more realistic to find people who can be supportive in the particular areas of your life that need support. Some people may prove ideal supporters in work-related issues, others in recreation, and still others in matters of romance.

NEGOTIATE FOR WIN-WIN

Try to understand how the needs and situation of your loved ones will be affected by your decisions. By knowing what motivates them, you'll be more able to win their support for the new actions you are considering.

People, in general—and your loved ones in particular—are motivated by power, security, money, love, sex, vanity, and fear. Your ability to get the things you need depends on your ability to *trade.* You offer certain things in your possession to motivate others to give you the things you want in return. Success depends largely on determining the specifics of this trading arrangement. That is, you must know what you need, who to trade with, what will motivate them to trade with you (their needs and desires), and what you are willing to trade in return.

This assessment is not a moral judgment; it's simply how the world is. It is easy to deceive yourself about this. Having an ongoing and long-established relationship with another person does not automatically guarantee that they'll support you in decisions offering few or no advantages to them.

INCLUDE YOUR LOVED ONES
IN YOUR DECISION

- Talk with them! Be open to their feelings and thoughts. Tell them candidly how you feel about the issues.

- Ask for their help.

- Consider how your obligations to them affect the decision.

- Consider how their obligations to you affect the decision.

- To gain support for your decision, show how it benefits them. Sometimes, the benefits may be indirect, such as having a happier and more fulfilled "you" to live with. At other times, you'll have to provide more direct benefits.

- If you make a decision that reduces the amount of emotional or financial support you're currently providing, expect resistance and counter-moves.

- Negotiate to overcome resistance. ("What would it take to get you to go along with this?") Expect to trade additional benefits in return for sacrifices or concessions on their part.

- Smoke out those who insist you cannot change or those who are totally unwilling to negotiate. Develop plans that allow you to pursue your decision in spite of their resistance.

GET EXPERT ADVICE IN SPECIAL CASES

Including others in your decisions helps you gain their insight and experience while you are evaluating your options. Those near to you may not be experts in the subject on which your decision rests. Yet, they may be able to offer insights that otherwise would elude you, simply because they don't have your habitual modes of perception.

The corresponding disadvantage of taking such advice from friends, family, priests, and coworkers is that they will look at your decision through *their* habitual modes of perception. They will filter your problem through their consciousness and values. Sometimes, this difference in perspectives leads to very useful insights. In other cases, it leads you astray. In good conscience, your advisors may tell you precisely the wrong thing to do.

The advice of people who are knowledgeable in the decision matter at hand can be extremely valuable. Experts *already* understand how things work, what the trade-offs are, and which resources, abilities, and conditions may be required. They can judge which issues are relevant, and which are not. Varied and substantial experience in their field gives them the conceptual ability to size up your situation quickly. They know what can go wrong, what precautions to take, what specific remedies are useful, and how to enhance promising options further.

> A businessman went to his doctor to complain of bulging eyes and a ringing in his ears. The doctor diagnosed the difficulty as due to high blood pressure and prescribed blood pressure pills. After a month, however, there was no improvement.
>
> He went to a second physician, who concluded that the man's teeth were the problem. They needed to be extracted. Yet, after the extraction, the condition persisted.
>
> The businessman was alarmed by now and sought the help of a third doctor. The doctor gave him a complete physical and took many blood samples. He concluded that the businessman had a rare blood disease that would be fatal within six months.
>
> The businessman wanted to make the best of his last six months, so he decided to take a luxury cruise around the world. He got the finest accommodations, the best luggage, the costliest new suits, and new leather shoes. For the first time in his life, he ordered custom-made shirts as well. The tailor measured him.
>
> "Let's see," said the tailor. "Sleeve thirty-three; collar sixteen."
>
> "Fifteen," countered the businessman.
>
> "Beg your pardon," said the tailor, "but I measure sixteen."

"Look here," said the man, "I've always worn a fifteen collar."

"Okay," said the tailor, "But don't say I didn't warn you. If you continue to wear a fifteen, your eyes are going to bulge out and there will be a ringing in your ears."

Okay, finding expert advice is not as easy as it might seem.[1] Usually, you will not know the individual personally, yet you must determine whether they can do the job for you. The difficulty is, they are the one with the knowledge, and you are the one with the problem! How can you figure out if they can help you, when you lack the very means to judge their proficiency? Fortunately, intuition and common sense can assist you. Ask yourself:

- Does the person have firsthand experience in the subject of interest?

- Is the person credible? Do others you know trust this person?

- Does the person stand to gain by advising you one way or the other, other than the fee that you might be paying them?

- Are they part of a group whose opinion on the matter is already decided? (For example, if you go to an antiabortion activist for advice about an unwanted pregnancy, you'll get their predetermined answer.)

- Do they ask sufficient relevant questions to understand your situation?

- Do they establish a positive tone? Are they projecting their own optimism or pessimism into your situation?

- Can the person reason the decision from *your* values, not theirs? That is, can they mentally place themselves in your shoes?

- Do they "blow in the wind" and tell you that anything you want to do is feasible? It's not hard for a trained manipulator

---

[1] In case you think that the above story is far-fetched, here's a *true* variation: In 1925, at age 40, my grandfather was told by *five* different doctors that he had only one year to live. In 1965, my grandfather was still alive and doing well. In fact, at age 80, he developed an inclination to constant laughter. I asked him, "Grandpa, why are you always laughing?" He explained, "Over the years, one after another of those five doctors passed away. Two months ago, the last one died. I managed to outlive *all* the doctors who predicted my early demise."

to sense your inner wishes and then parrot them back to you. It gives you a warm feeling, but you won't profit from it.

■ Can the person explain the reasons for their recommendations to you?

■ Can they sketch out the process by which they arrived at their conclusions and advice?

■ Do they state the important conditions upon which they base their advice?

Having been a consultant (in mechanical engineering) for many years, I can assure you that there's an enormous difference among individual consultants. Despite the credentials that are proffered, some consultants are scatter-brained and incompetent, while others are insightful and effective.

Using experts to good effect requires that you monitor your progress with them and carefully explain your time and monetary limitations. If you meet up with a prima donna who is doing you a favor by just taking your money, or a frustrated preacher who doesn't really listen to you, move on to a different expert. Most important, always keep in mind this cardinal rule for using experts: Asking for advice does not oblige you to accept it.

> ## Asking for advice does not oblige you to accept it.

For many people, therapy is a very useful experience. It opens up new avenues of thinking and feeling in their lives. It encourages them to greater personal responsibility and fulfillment. Nevertheless, in the context of the present discussion, remember that *therapy is not advice.*

If you go into therapy with the idea that you'll receive help on a particular problem, you may be surprised. More often than not, therapists look beyond the problem you bring to them (the "presenting problem") and try to treat the underlying personality disorder. In fact, the problem you present to them may only be a metaphor for a much more pervasive problem in your life.

I make no claims about the efficacy of psychological treatment other than to say that many surveys show that it has mixed results. About one-third of the surveyed patients felt therapy was useful, one-third felt it had no observable effects, and one-third claimed it actually made things worse or undermined their self-esteem.

Because therapy treats the underlying personality problem, do not expect a decision to emerge painlessly from therapy. To the contrary, it's quite possible that therapy may make you feel even more anxious or confused! As certain unflattering psychological facts emerge in the dialogue, you may feel more distressed than when you started. You may become aware that the decision challenges facing you are even greater than you had initially acknowledged.

If you feel unbearably anxious about a major decision, by all means, see a qualified psychologist or psychiatrist. But do not enter therapy with the idea that the psychologist will make your decisions for you or give you permission to do what you want. (One sign of no longer *needing* a psychologist is that you have given up this expectation.)

THE PERILS OF DECISION BY CONSENSUS

The Miller, His Son, and Their Donkey

A miller and his son were walking on the road to town with their donkey. They encountered a group of women and children who called after the miller, "Shame on you! You're making your poor boy walk when he can barely keep up." So the miller put his son on the donkey and they continued.

A little while later, they came upon an old man who chastised the son, "How can you make your poor father walk when you are young and energetic?" So the son encouraged his father to mount the donkey in his place and they resumed their trip.

Soon after, they met two hunters who taunted the miller, "You fool! If your donkey can carry you, it can also handle your son." So the father reached down and set his son behind him on the donkey.

A few miles later, they came to a bridge. The passers-by sneered at them, "You cruel oafs! Why are you riding that poor donkey? It's so old and weak, *you* should be carrying it." So the father and son dismounted and prepared to carry the donkey. In lifting the donkey onto their shoulders, however, they moved too close to the edge of the bridge and lost their footing. The donkey toppled into the river and was drowned.

The moral of this story: No matter how much advice you receive, the responsibility for taking it is yours.

Some decisions are best not made by a group, yet sometimes a group may be asked to decide something about you. For example, a social club may decide whether to admit you, a thesis committee may pass judgment on your research abilities, or your country may decide to send you to a foreign land to fight a war. Do not confuse *their* decision for *your* decision. You can decide to abide by their decision, reject their decision, or find other alternatives outside its scope. What's good for the group as a whole may not be good for you individually.

The decision-making process of groups is a fascinating psychological study area.[2] A group is composed of people with different values, backgrounds, priorities, talents, and education. Some members welcome change for its own sake, whereas others want to maintain stability at all costs. Some are willing to invest generously in the future, while others value current profitability more highly. Some are optimistic about the future and the group's ability to navigate change. Others are pessimistic and worry that the group may lack the resources or ability to weather upcoming storms.

Most important, each person brings to the group his or her own personal stakes in the decision. For any particular decision, some people will come out ahead, others will be unaffected, and some will come out behind. It is not necessarily a *zero-sum game*, in which the gains of the winners equals the losses of the losers. In group decision making, sometimes everybody loses; sometimes everybody wins. Most often, the situation lies between these two extremes, so that different people in the group have their own motives for acting as they do.

---

[2] See Irving L. Janis's *Victims of Groupthink* (1972) for a compelling account of how independent critical thinking can be undermined by "groupthink." The book considers U.S. foreign policy decisions such as the Bay of Pigs fiasco and the Vietnam war from the viewpoint of group psychological processes.

Because of these underlying splits in the group's psyche, it's unrealistic to expect that a group knows what is best for you or *even for itself*. It doesn't matter whether the group is your family, your employer, your church, or your bowling club; take their advice with a grain of salt. The group's decision may include the individual members' folly and exclude their individual wisdom.

USE ROLE MODELS AND NETWORKING

Role models provide concrete images of your goals. They're a living example of the situations to which you aspire. Role models are valuable because they allow you to visualize the rewards of that situation, as well as the necessary effort and trade-offs. They encourage you to mold your efforts accordingly.

For many years, I have hung portraits of my personal heroes on the wall of my study. These pictures are a constant reminder of my goals. They show me that certain situations to which I aspire *are* possible.

Living role models are even better. Find people who are already doing what you want to do. Create a context to meet them. Can you join the club they belong to, or the same professional society, or be introduced through mutual friends?

Another good way to gain support is *networking*, which is the informal process of talking to people you know to contact people you don't know. It extends your personal horizons. You simply ask friends, family, coworkers, business associates, neighbors, and fellow club and church members if they know someone who can help you find the information or assistance you need. Networking works best when you are very specific about what you are looking for.

Networking is talking to people you *do* know in order to contact people you *don't* know.

Ten years ago, I was having lunch with Steve, a business friend. During our conversation, Steve mentioned he had heard secondhand that the ABC Company was looking for a consultant in my technical specialty. I asked him if he knew anyone at ABC, but he didn't.

When I returned, I called Bob, the only person I knew at ABC. I queried, "Do you know the group or project within your company that needs a consultant in my field?"

Bob responded, "Hmmm, I don't. Let me ask around."

Two days later, Bob called back. He said, "I've asked half a dozen friends here. None of them knows of any such project. You must be confusing us with another company."

I was humiliated and gave up. Bob was my only contact at ABC—or so I thought. Two days went by. While taking a shower, I remembered that I had another friend, Frank, who was not working at ABC, but who was involved in the same technical area. I called Frank. He didn't know which new projects they were starting either. Then he said, "Wait, I know Ollie, ABC's director of research, very well. If anyone knew, it would be Ollie. Just tell him I told you to call."

I called Ollie and introduced myself as a friend of Frank's. I quickly went on to say I was a consultant specializing in fluid mechanics and gave him a half-minute summary of my background. I continued, "I hear that a group within ABC is seeking consulting help in my exact specialty. Could you verify this and direct me to the right project?"

Ollie laughed and said, "My, news does travel fast. Yes, the project you are referring to is our brand new laser project. Why don't you call Jim P., the project manager, and see what he has to say?"

I called Jim P. and talked for twenty minutes. Indeed, there *was* a need for my technical specialty. Jim P. invited me to submit a proposal on the work. One month later, I landed a very lucrative contract with ABC. . . . Networking pays!

The key concept in networking is *participation.* You must be part of the game in order to win benefits. You must be seen, heard, and felt. It takes more than a single chance meeting for networking to work well. Just as in the advertising game, repetition counts. Frequent contact builds connections which, eventually, will open the doors to new opportunities.

I never cease to be amazed at the unpredictable and spontaneous ways such connections work. For example, in my consulting work, I am always looking for opportunities to write technical papers. Once I was participating on a committee to prepare some reliability guidelines for a particular product. After three or four meetings, I developed a good rapport with one of the other participants. He complained, "What we need is a good way to assess the effects of elevated temperatures on reliability, but we don't know how to do it."

I recognized his complaint as an opportunity to write a technical paper addressing that very issue. I explained my experience in that field and volunteered to write a guideline. Three months later, I had written a valuable technical paper *and* solved an important problem for that company.

Networking can be overdone. It's possible, in some situations, to exhaust the goodwill of your friends this way. Most people, however, tend to the other extreme: They underutilize networking. They discover that they could have asked a friend to introduce them to a useful contact, but they were afraid to impose. They feel that networking will turn them into glad-handing opportunists or social gadflies. On the contrary, networking allows you to tap the valuable "people resources" right at your fingertips. You will discover that most people are only too glad to help you, especially if it's at no cost to themselves.

Networking requires keeping track of old friends and acquaintances, as well as volunteering for new committees and groups. In general, circulate more. Because you'll need something more to offer than a handshake, try to be judicious in your choice of contacts, or you'll quickly overextend yourself.

Successful networking usually pays back benefits in a relatively short time. If you're maintaining relationships where you are always giving benefits, but never receiving them, it's time for some house cleaning. Another rule of thumb: For every two beneficial contacts gained, discard one old contact that has proven fruitless.

An important aspect of networking is spending time with people who are in a similar situation. If you want to become an artist, start associating with artists. If you want to become more adept at computers, join a local computer user's group. The energy you will gain through these associations cannot be underestimated. Common goals are a very strong bond between people.

Friends may wish you well, but they're no substitute for people who are in the same situation. The latter already know what your options are about and can offer useful advice about the trade-offs you might have to make. Their listening is different from the listening of those who are not in the same situation. You don't have to explain every small oddity of your situation to them. They *know* the implications of each of your options because they have "lived the options" themselves. But, most important, you don't have to feel like an ugly duckling with these people. You're in the same boat, and they will have more compassion toward your situation. You belong.

In my consulting, I found it very beneficial to associate with other consultants. I discovered this quite by accident. Occasionally I would meet other consultants at a client's facility, and a natural affinity was often apparent. We would arrange to meet for lunch, and often a friendship would result. I discovered that other consultants were asking the same kinds of questions that concerned me. The insight I gained from the way they made their decisions helped me in my own.

In a manner of speaking, I was able to extend my own experience by listening to theirs. These fellow consultants were very generous with their time and energy in helping me. Their practical advice bolstered my business position and saved me a ton of frustration.

I'd like to end this chapter with some parting observations:

■ You can discover who can be supportive only by asking for support and seeing what happens.

■ *Pay* for your support. It's a two-way street, so be generous in supporting others.

■ If you are looking for support in a very narrow context, expect to search far and wide.

■ Have something in common with your supporters.

■ Understand the different kinds and levels of support.

■ Many support groups are often anything but supportive. They may be full of people who are all looking for a lift from others without having the psychological energy to give anyone else a lift.

■ It's easy to recognize when someone has a supportive attitude. They want you to win, they see you as capable, and they accept you as you are.

9

CONQUER WISHFUL THINKING

REALITY-TEST YOUR DECISIONS

Decision making is not 100 percent objective, like mathematics. Nor is it 100 percent subjective, like story telling. Decision making is a chameleon that shifts back and forth between these two polarities.

The subjective part of decision making deals with inner (psychological) reality. You imagine a project and consider the actions necessary to make it happen in the world as a material fact.

The objective part of decision making starts with (outer) material reality. You observe what is happening "out there" and react accordingly. The world outside you (the "environment") places demands and limitations on your actions. Learning "how things work" in the environment is an important part of the objective dimension of decision making. It allows you to adapt your strategies to the way the world works. As your actions unfold, you can measure their impact and then modify the strategies.

Decision making connects subjective imagination and objective testing in an endless chain:

Imagine —> Test —> Imagine —> Test —> ...

Because decision making is a form of learning, it must be *practiced* to become effective. With experience, you improve your judgment about

- What you can accomplish
- How things work in the world
- What strategies are useful for you

Reality testing a decision does not refer exclusively to external reality, but also to inner reality. It is concerned not only with how things work in the external world, but also with how they work subjectively. Success is defined by how *you* value the results of your decisions.

Reality testing is an essential part of decision making. Without it, you're setting yourself up for disappointment. You'll learn what the world's limitations are, but at the expense of feeling powerless in your own life. Without a good mental model of how your efforts and attitudes will be received by others, you'll be unable to plan effectively and to reap the benefits of your actions.

Here are some basic rules for staying in touch with reality while making decisions. They will help you assess your self, your environment, your situation, and your plans more accurately:

1. Do not confuse past with present.

2. Do not confuse wish with fact.

3. Do not confuse other people's opinions of your abilities or resources for reality.

4. Do not confuse another person's ability to accomplish a goal for your own.

5. Do not confuse another person's situation for your own.

6. Do not confuse idle promises for firm commitments.

7. Do not confuse your enthusiasm or motivation for a project with that of another person.

BALANCE PLANNING AND PERFORMANCE

People who are adept at planning are not necessarily adept at implementing the very plans they conceive. Conversely, many people are better at executing plans that others have established than coming up with their own plans. Business recognizes this natural disparity in individual abilities and lets workers gravitate to the end to which their personality is suited. There are vice presidents of research, development, and strategic planning. There are vice presidents of administration and operations. And rarely the twain shall meet. Yet, on an individual level, it is very important to discover which ability needs work, and conscientiously set out to strengthen it. When it comes to your own life and your own decisions, you must accept both of these commonly disparate roles (planner and performer) for yourself if you are to be truly responsible for your own actions.

Planning is essential in gathering information, analyzing trends, considering alternatives, and coordinating resources. Without planning, performance is mere busyness: There is no measure of how well the activity is satisfying the goal.

Impulsive decision makers jump right in without any planning whatsoever and later rationalize their hastiness by blaming poor outcomes on outside factors. Impulsive decision makers like to point to all the change they have carried out, to all the new action. In their haste to produce these changes, they fail to acknowledge that the resulting changes often bring no improvement, that they bring them no closer to their goals. These men and women of action suffer from a mistaken belief that *any* action is better than no action. They mistrust their own planning ability and try to cover their weaknesses up with a flurry of activity.

> # Do not confuse *activity* with *progress*.

Excessive activity is often used to cover up a fear of planning. Individuals who busy themselves with constant activity never allow themselves the time to recognize that certain needs are presently unmet. They do not have to deal with the effort of planning. They can avoid the risk of making concrete plans and then falling short. They distract themselves by creating fire drills, attending needless meetings, traveling too much, and working on unimportant details. They *appear* to be making progress, but they are getting nowhere fast.

On the other hand, *performance* is also crucial. In both business and personal arenas, many people use information gathering and planning as a means of procrastinating. They engage in an endless series of meetings to define and analyze a problem, describe the pros and cons, but can't integrate the emerging facts into coherent action. These planning actions do not fully address the real issues facing them. They consider how things work "on paper" without also testing their effect in the outside world. This kind of ineffective performance makes them more vulnerable to negative forces in the environment.

ALL PLANNING	ALL PERFORMANCE
(The "dreamer")	(The "busybody")
■ Immersed in information gathering, worrying, analyzing, "preparing," and endless talking about what they're going to do.	■ Impulsively acts without concern for consequences. Feels that activity is the sole measure of progress.
■ Never tests the plan.	■ Never plans the test.
■ Can set goals, but can't actualize them.	■ Gets "things" done, but not those that correspond to their goals.

Effective decision makers balance planning and performance. One key to successful decision making is to avoid being stuck at either end of this spectrum. Put on your planning cap when planning is required, and put on your worker's cap when it's time to roll up your sleeves and set your plan into action.

RESIST THE SUBTLE HYPNOSIS
OF ESCAPE DREAMS

We all know the kind of person who has difficulty making decisions. They seem to take forever to make up their minds. When circumstances finally force them to a course of action, they feel anxious and desperate. They're uncomfortable either way: Leaving the old situation is painful; entering the new situation is equally painful.

In the past thirty years, psychologists have given much study to the processes by which indecision arises. They've come up with a surprising result: People *learn* indecisiveness at a very early age.

Parents who are too strict or demanding create the atmosphere in which indecision is bred. In many authoritarian families, the child is not allowed to express his or her own inclinations. The child learns to stifle his or her own instincts in favor of obedience. The child is rewarded for obedience, that is, *ignoring* his or her own will. The youngster learns—at an unconscious level—that the price of parental love is giving up his or her sense of self.

The child is faced with an unspoken dilemma: If the child acts on his or her own impulses, the chances of being punished are high. If the child is obedient, he or she will be "loved," but only at the price of denying his or her own inclinations. The youngster must repress the normal aggressive energies that are part of a fully functioning person. To manage this, the "too obedient" child introjects the severe rule maker and turns all normal and acceptable aggression toward itself. When this young person grows to adulthood, problems arise whenever conflict or resistance is encountered. The person cannot muster the assertiveness needed to meet the challenge. Instead, they channel the outward aggression into self-denial, self-disparagement, self-doubt, and *indecision*.

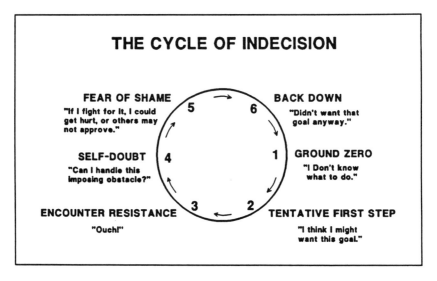

THE CYCLE OF INDECISION

The too obedient person finds it easier to *dream* about goals than to take action to fulfill them. Wishful thinking allows overly obedient people to remain captive to the *cycle of indecision.* At the first sign of opposition or conflict in pursuing their goal, they cannot summon the aggressive energies required to maintain their path. They back down rather than display self-assertion or acceptable aggression. To act aggressively—even when justified—brings into consciousness their old fear: Displaying self-assertion, anger, or force will make them unlovable. They avoid this situation at all costs.

Another form of escape is used by people with a thin skin who lack the ego-strength to deal with the trials of everyday life. They cannot admit this to themselves, however, so they invent an excuse: They didn't really want that goal or have that need. This excuse reenacts the same defense they unconsciously used as a child. The thin-skinned withdraw from the fray and deny their own interests.

Intellectually, thin-skinned people know that losing will not destroy their inner self. *Emotionally,* they still equate losing with total destruction. When they're in a game of Monopoly and losing badly, thin-skinned people secretly wish that their game piece (metaphorically representing their inner self) would disappear. Thus removed from the game, their inner self does not have to experience the pain and humiliation of losing.

Success for the thin-skinned is *never losing.* All conscious and explicit goals are undermined by an unconscious process that constantly observes how much loss is possible, how that loss can be minimized, and whether safety (invulnerability) can be maintained. The psychic energy needed to maintain this constant vigilance drains off positive energy that can be used to further the stated goal. When resistance occurs, they abandon the goal, often in subtle ways. One common method is disengaging the inner self from the process before a loss could annihilate it. They go through the motions on the outside, but on the inside, they've already given up.

Ironically, excessive sensitivity to losing virtually *guarantees* continued losing! Eventually all (nontrivial) projects encounter some form of resistance. When they do, excessive sensitivity to losing makes it seem "safer" to abandon the project. Yet, abandoning the project constitutes a larger loss: You never reach the goals you want.

A more subtle form of escape dream occurs when you get involved with people who benefit from "preparing" you for a new situation. For example, many schools advertise to teach you how to earn a handsome income by writing children's stories, painting portraits, or running a massage studio. These schools offer encouragement while they're taking your money. As soon as you're on your own, the encouragement stops. There is nothing wrong or bad about this situation, but it's important to realize that you were *buying* your strokes. You were receiving a biased feedback in your reality testing.

Excessive sensitivity to losing virtually *guarantees* continued losing.

If you have some of this psychological background, do not despair. There's a simple antidote: *Learn to take and give punches.*

Learning to take punches means developing greater frustration tolerance. By gaining the courage to enter the fray rather than escape from it, you will learn experientially that losing does not destroy you. Further, you'll discover that losing doesn't make you unlovable. Finally, you'll be able to give up the burden of always looking over your shoulder for imminent disaster.

In learning to take punches, you'll also discover that exposing yourself (taking off the masks you have to wear for the various roles you must play to function in a complex society) will not necessarily ruin you. You may wonder, "Will people still love, respect, and accept me if I take the mask off? Will they appreciate me if I stop hiding certain aspects of myself?" Although the answer in many situations is "No," it's common for us to generalize it incorrectly to *all* situations. By keeping the masks on all the time, we starve our reality and fatten our unreality.

Only when we accept the risk of exposing our inner side do we discover, bit by bit, that there *are* issues and people with whom we must take the chance and put aside the masks. By learning to say who we are and to fight *openly* for it, we bring our full power to the fray. By not trying to fight from behind a mask, the energy required to carry the mask around can be applied directly to the contest.

Learning to give punches means recognizing the validity of justifiable assertiveness. Justifiable assertiveness is not pushiness or egoism, but a positive form of aggression that helps you to ask for the things you need and makes you aware that you must be willing to compete or trade for them. Fair fighting is a necessary part of life—*everyone's* life. Fair fighting helps you at:

- Work, by letting you feel better about self-promotion and marketing what you have to offer.

- Romance, by allowing you to insist on fair treatment. It helps you confront your partner with a request to negotiate instead of simply making demands or acquiescing to your partner's demands.

- Friendships, by leading you to choose better. You learn that saying "no" will not necessarily fracture a solid relationship.

- Life in general, by making you aware that things will not happen unless *you* enter the fray. You are the agent of change in your own life. The person who waits to be saved or for "something to happen" sits by the side of the boxing ring and gives up responsibility for themselves.

Most books on stress management emphasize *coping* skills (learning to take punches). They advise you contain, defuse, or otherwise adapt your emotional responses to stressful events. Yet, relaxation, meditation, and autosuggestion will take you only so far. There are many situations in which prolonged coping leads to a sense of powerlessness and frustration.

I think there's much merit in the opposite approach: Manage stress by giving punches. This method of managing stress says, "Get tough! Don't let the bastards grind you down. Push back. Summon your aggressive energies." Fair fighting is an *active* approach to stress reduction. To be sure, fair fighting carries some risks. Usually, however, accepting the challenge this way is healthy and appropriate, because you experience yourself as an active agent rather than as a person who passively accommodates.

Learning to give and take punches is a form of "ego weight lifting." Engagement in the fray builds up your confidence, skill, courage, and ability to handle opposition. In short, it builds up *you*.

A strong ego is developed by experiencing yourself as powerful. This does not mean that you become all powerful—like Superman or Wonder Woman—but merely equal to the tasks set before you. Being powerful means that external situations don't completely define you. Instead, you can muster the psychological strength to attain your goals in the midst of the external situation. This book, it is hoped, will help you access that stronger *you*.

TRADE WITH THE ENVIRONMENT TO SATISFY YOUR NEEDS

The key to conquering wishful thinking is to become more and more able to extract the support you need *from the environment*. If your dreams cannot provide the support you need, you'll be forced to try to "live" within them. (This is the Gestalt definition of neurosis.) Thus, it's important to discern whether your decision brings you benefits in the real world or merely decorates pipe dreams about yourself.

Many people confuse wants with needs. They ignore their real needs and tell themselves that their *wants* are *needs*. That is, they set up false needs while depriving themselves of their real needs. What are these real needs?

- Adequate food and shelter
- Exercise
- Love
- Social relatedness
- Income
- Self-esteem
- Safety
- Meaning

What are some wants that are often perceived as needs?

- Fame
- High income
- Status
- Talent
- Beauty
- Accomplishment
- Desire for an elegant car or house

Goals can correspond to fulfilling either wants or needs. Therefore, merely setting and pursuing goals isn't the whole story. If you do not meet at least some of your real needs while you're pursuing your "want" goals, you'll shrivel up or go crazy. Keeping your eyes exclusively on your "wants" is dangerous. Attainment of the *wants*—however worthy or desirable—does not guarantee that your *needs* will be met.

Needs are always satisfied in relationship to the environment. If you cannot—or are unwilling to—trade to get what you require from the world at large, you are depriving yourself. Or, you may even deny that you have certain needs, thereby avoiding the feeling of disappointment if they are not satisfied.

Some people would rather withdraw than state their needs. Stating their needs makes them feel vulnerable. They quietly hope that somebody will magically guess their needs, much as their mother anticipated their every need when they were one year old. Other people manage to state their needs, but are unwilling to trade appropriately to satisfy them. They're reluctant to pay the required price or to follow the rules of the trading

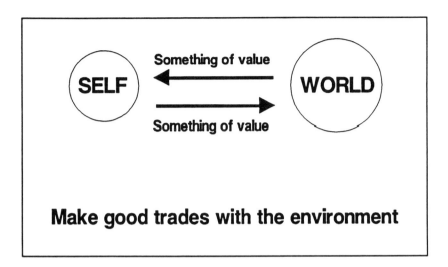

Make good trades with the environment

game. Their desire to dictate the terms of the trade disregards the nature of the marketplace in which their needs could be satisfied. They become discouraged: Although they try harder and harder, the goal seems to get farther and farther away.

The Gestalt interpretation of this situation is illuminating. Such people are *contacting* the environment incorrectly.[1] It's not a matter of trying harder. They must *try differently*. You must contact the environment in a way that gets the outcomes you want. If you are not getting the results you want, then change your strategies, criteria, methods, or trading partners—until you find something that does work.

An important corollary to this principle: If nobody wants to trade for the things you are offering, offer *something else*. The deal that nobody wants is like a useless currency. It may say, "Worth one million dollars," but no one will honor it in a trade. Part of feeling powerful in everyday life is knowing that you can offer things that will motivate others to trade with you.

---

[1] *Environment* is a general notion. In some contexts, it corresponds to *local* situations such as living in a particular city or state, being in a certain profession or business organization, or being part of your parent's family. There are many small "ponds" within the overall environment, and it is important to find out *which* ponds are right for you.

THE PSYCHOLOGICAL ORIGINS
OF WISHFUL THINKING

Pursuing *wants* to the exclusion of real needs results in poor trading with the environment. The unbalanced elevation of wants over needs is characteristic of a very common personality disorder called narcissism.[2] The narcissist *wants* to be a great professional athlete, musician, writer, scientist, or wealthy investor—but doesn't give a hoot about satisfying real needs. Attaining fame, they feel, will make up for the sacrifice of their real needs.

One area in which these distinctions play a significant role is that of work choices. (See the two figures on the facing page.) A mature and well-adjusted person sees that "meaningful work" not only provides benefits to self, but also to the employer or the market. It's a good trade with the environment.

The narcissistic person, on the other hand, seeks the "perfect" job, one that ideally suits his or her talents and in which he or she will be asked to do *only* those things that enhance his or her own progress and image. The narcissistic person observes that most "real" work (that is, most jobs available in the marketplace) does not decorate the grandiose self in this way. Plain old work is secretly devalued.

The external world cannot value the narcissist in the extravagant way that would make him happy. The narcissist insists, "Everything I want to do pays little or nothing; everything that pays adequately is of no interest to me."

Meaningful work is never found using these mutually exclusive categories, so the narcissist plans a "creative" career—one characterized by escape and lack of trading with the environment to get real needs satisfied. These efforts are usually unsuccessful because they don't provide sufficient value to the environment. The way out of the dilemma is not for the narcissist to "decide" more intelligently, but to work (therapeutically and experientially) on the self-other boundary. What does this mean in practice?

---

[2] See *Humanizing the Narcissistic Style* by Stephen M. Johnson (1987) for a readable and empathetic discussion of narcissism and its therapeutic treatment.

CONQUER WISHFUL THINKING

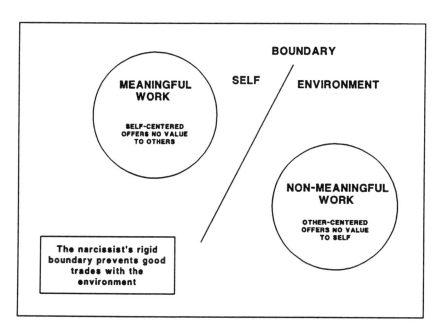

BOUNDARY

SELF | **ENVIRONMENT**

MEANINGFUL WORK

SELF-CENTERED
OFFERS NO VALUE
TO OTHERS

NON-MEANINGFUL WORK

OTHER-CENTERED
OFFERS NO VALUE
TO SELF

The narcissist's rigid boundary prevents good trades with the environment

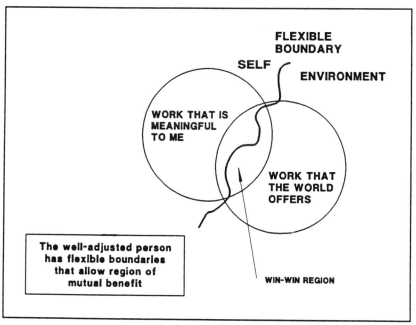

FLEXIBLE BOUNDARY

SELF

ENVIRONMENT

WORK THAT IS MEANINGFUL TO ME

WORK THAT THE WORLD OFFERS

The well-adjusted person has flexible boundaries that allow region of mutual benefit

WIN-WIN REGION

1. The grandiose self must come down out of its ivory tower of fussiness and self-sufficiency and learn where the self-other boundary (that is, the trading boundary) really is. From the outside, it looks as if the grandiose self asks too much of the environment. We all know people like this: They expect others to support their cause without giving sufficient return on the demanded investment. They extend their hand for others to affirm them, but then find it difficult to affirm others. They feel that because they're immersed in a high-priority project, they are *excused* from the rules of the trading game. They want special treatment.

2. The grandiose self must replace the unrealistic expectation of finding the perfect situation with the expectation of finding an *adequate* one, one that also provides benefits to the environment.

3. The unworthy self—which is the shadow side of the grandiose self—must learn to feel *safe* enough to start trading with the environment. The unworthy self can be thought of as the fragile ego of the child within. The fragile ego has to learn that trading with the environment entails some risk of being misused, manipulated, or *hurt*. The unworthy self learns to bear these possibilities by experiencing that giving benefits to the environment does not necessarily result in personal loss.

Many people have been hurt as a result of prior manipulation. They feel the need to protect themselves from future harm at all costs. Yet, there is a price in belonging to groups and in establishing trading relations with others. It is putting yourself in a situation where you can be manipulated.

On an intellectual level, the issue of manipulation is rarely a problem. It's part of trading and cannot be avoided. It is, instead, on the *feeling* level that being manipulated is troublesome. Emotionally, being manipulated reminds us of being helpless and vulnerable. When we enter a trade that has some aspect of risk, the unconscious mind sends a message, "Danger, you may be manipulated." Never being manipulated pushes us away from trading with the environment to the "safety" of isolation. By abstaining from trade, we protect the fragile ego from being destroyed by a bad deal, but never allow ourself to gain real benefits.

Protecting yourself at the cost of never gaining real benefits is a poor strategy. A better strategy is to develop strength and flexibility: Become strong enough to resist harmful environmental effects yet flexible enough to adapt when required.

The rigid personality rebounds like a billiard ball from one survival situation to the next. For such a person, life always looks difficult; existence is always struggle, struggle. Too much inflexibility leads to tension. To release accumulated strains, worries, and ego bruises, the rigid person needs to become more resilient. The secret of flexibility lies in gaining a deeper sense of self-acceptance and integration. The potential energy used to hold the self together in the midst of crisis ("bracing against the storm") is transformed into kinetic energy, the fluid motion of self-expression ("going with the wind").

The person who has been hurt greatly in the past becomes hypervigilant. They're too quick to anticipate and ward off possible hurts in the future. The price of being *too* vigilant is that you never relax. The spontaneous flow of emotions ceases. You're always thinking in terms of problems and maintaining your defenses so as to maximize personal safety. This sensitivity leads to the inability to *absorb* frustration and small hurts. Everything must be responded to. Flexibility helps you cope better with fears of being hurt.

4. The grandiose self must learn to *pay the price*. The narcissist would like to offer his or her own version of what a good trade is. Learning to pay the price starts with feeling, "I am worth it. If I really need something, I have to accept the going rate. To refuse to pay the going price is to deny my own worth, to deny that I need that thing. Further, paying the price entitles me to some assurances as a consumer. I get to choose what I want and have a reasonable right of return if the goods are not as advertised. That is, I have the right to ask of the trade certain concessions that are responsive to *my* needs."

The narcissist tries to manipulate trades so as to maintain an artificial advantage. He tries to buy everything for 20 cents on the dollar. He's a sucker for bargains that do not satisfy his real needs. He chooses situations that have a high payoff (be it in terms of money, status, position, or favors) without regard for his real needs. He is fooled by promises of secret methods, shortcuts, and lazy person's approaches.

The narcissist refuses to collect the ordinary credentials to do the kind of work he desires, and instead seeks a magical shortcut to bypass the effort that others must exert. Ordinary preparation is devalued; the world must be taken by storm. The grandiose self sets itself a task equal to the "impossible dream," which is doomed to failure almost from the start. The grandiose self will not admit a simple truth: If a goal is really worth it, it is also worth taking the time to get there. One must pick up the necessary supplies and credentials to make a journey.

> 5. The fragile self must learn good judgment by experience. The small child in a candy store does not have enough sense of self to choose wisely. Instead, he or she chooses those sweets that make the biggest claim on his or her attention. (The sweets "choose" the child!)

A small child cannot make wise choices because he or she is partially unaware of his or her own needs and values. Further, the child lacks the discrimination to see when those needs are being satisfied. More importantly, the child cannot see the environment as it is, in order to make good distinctions about the true nature of the trade. A youngster is easily misled by a con man, a joker, or a hypocrite because the youngster cannot yet distinguish the offered reality from the underlying reality. Adults do analogous things when they engage in wishful thinking: They ignore vitally important aspects of the situation that contradict what they want to see.

> 6. The grandiose self must avoid confusing the issue of ability with the issue of satisfying real needs. This confusion distracts the grandiose self from noticing the pain of not meeting its needs in the here-and-now.

For the narcissist, talent and ability are rarely the issue. Most narcissists have a superabundance of talent. Rather, it's the way they go about things; they set themselves up for failure. They set nearly impossible tasks to themselves. If they succeed, society pronounces them heroes (maybe). If they fail, no one can blame or shame them for it, since the task was so difficult in the first place. In this manner, the narcissist structures all efforts so as to never face the pain of losing. The real goal of the narcissist is "not losing" instead of "winning."

FIND ACCEPTABLE CHOICES

Finding acceptable choices is not easy for anyone, by virtue of the fact that we are all so unique. But instead of trying to find the perfect match, you can save yourself much heartache by satisficing: Try to find situations that are "good enough." Forget about finding the marriage partner with movie star looks, Einstein-level IQ, or prima ballerina talent. Instead, concentrate on finding someone who has reasonably compatible attributes, values, and interests. Forget about finding the ultimate career position, in terms of prestige, power, and salary. Instead, concentrate on finding reasonable situations that also consider the people environment and whether the work is meaningful.

In making acceptable choices, set realistic *minimum* criteria to avoid the polar opposite of grandiosity: self-denial. Eliminate those choices that serve only as vehicles to act out self-hating tendencies. Be careful not to punish yourself by insisting that you make a decision or discover an alternative that will suddenly and magically resolve all your problems and frustrations. Instead, be gentle with yourself. At the same time, try to develop new insight and actions that support growth and encourage realistic goals. By affirming yourself, being compassionate to yourself, and feeling your own worth, you will find yourself making better choices.

Searches for the optimal or "elegant" solution to your problem are usually a form of self-punishment. Frequently, such elegant solutions are the very ones that make you an instant genius, authority, or superstar. The elusive search for the elegant solution is food that the grandiose self dangles in front of the real self. The real self remains hungry. It needs food, even if it is ordinary!

Some people vacillate between the extremes of grandiosity ("*No* situation is good enough") and self-deprecation ("*Any* choice is acceptable; I don't deserve better"). The self-denying voice insists that you're desperate and that you should take the first opportunity that comes along: the first person, group, or company that accepts you. In such situations, you are neither optimizing nor satisficing, but *minimizing* (= begging = self-hating).

The elusive search for the elegant solution is food that the grandiose self dangles in front of the real self.

Constant doubts about your present alternative are another form of self-punishment. These doubts often mean, "You don't deserve the goal you've chosen." The effect is paralyzed productivity and undermined confidence.

Evaluating the suitability of projects and opportunities requires both practical criteria and insight. The practical criteria are valuable in preventing desperate, self-hating choices, as well as in moderating grandiose ambitions. Insight is necessary to see the whole situation in evaluating its suitability. To some extent, we do not see the whole, but only those aspects that feed into our narcissistic deficits. We often see only what we want to see, and miss important negatives. This makes it easy to be attracted to a poor choice because of a single characteristic that we weight too highly. Similarly, we sometimes reject good choices due to a single minor fault.

Nowhere is this decision myopia more apparent than in the area of human relationships. It's much more common for us to deliberate on whether we are being accepted or rejected than to consider whether we are satisfying our needs within a relationship.

In something as intangible as a relationship, the key is to sense the underlying *rapport*. This requires a certain amount of discipline in observation. It's very easy to be distracted by approval, rejection, credentials, appearances, possessions, and what people *say* they're like. It's also easy to be misled by what you think *about the other person or group.*

There's a much more direct way to get at the truth: Simply be yourself in the interaction and carefully observe *how you feel about yourself.* (This little piece of advice can be worth a hundred times the price of this book!) Do you feel good about yourself as you experience the relationship? Do you feel capable, valuable, and comfortable? Or do you feel inadequate, out of place, or otherwise uneasy? This method allows great insight into whether that relationship is right for you.

10

MANAGE SETBACKS
AND UNCERTAINTY

MONITOR YOUR DECISION

Twenty-five hundred years ago, the Greek philosopher Heraclitus commented, "The only thing we can be sure of is *change*." The river that we step into now is not the same river that we stepped into last year. The water is different, the temperature is different, and even the shape of the bank is different due to erosion and accumulation of silt.

Fads and styles arise, take hold, peak, and then decline. Nations rise and fall. With takeover deals, giant corporations can appear or disappear overnight. Opinions, habits, and consumer preferences change. Even values and basic attitudes change. Just think of the changes that have occurred in the last century in our attitudes about abortion, slavery, women's rights, child labor, and the six-day workweek. Even the planet earth is changing. For thousands of years, the average temperature of the oceans has been rising. In a period as short as the last forty years, man's use of fluorocarbons has produced a noticeable change in the earth's ozone layer.

What does the fact of change have to do with decision making? A lot. As the world changes beneath our very feet, as we change, as our relationships change, as our ideas and values change—we find ourselves faced with the problem of how to adapt, how to factor the new "world" or the new "us" into our decisions.

Paying attention to change is vitally important. Adapting to change allows you to grow, survive, and even flourish. You may be wealthy, beautiful, or talented, but if you do not adapt to changing reality, your gifts may be wasted.

There's something inside us that would prefer the situation to be otherwise. As human beings, we love constancy and pre-dictability. We are creatures of habit, and to a large extent, we feel most comfortable with a stable environment.

An unstable, constantly changing environment is disorient-ing. If the world becomes too chaotic, we can't find our bearings or make intelligent plans. Rapid change—in ourselves or the world around us—generates many fears: We may not have enough time to react adequately. We may not recognize what is chal-lenging us. We may not know how to respond.

Change is always risky. Emotionally, when we're in the midst of rapid change, we batten down the hatches—brace our-selves—and go into survival mode. This generates enormous psychic tension. Since the extent of the challenge is not clear, we prepare ourselves for the worst that we can imagine.

Because we are so inclined by nature to embrace perma-nence, we like to think that once we have made a decision, that's it. We can let the matter drop. We won't have to go through the anxiety of deciding again. Although such thoughts may be comforting, they can lead us astray. A more useful perspective can be gained by restating Heraclitus' observation in decision making terminology:

MOST DECISIONS ARE NOT "FOREVER"

1. Situations change.
2. Your goals evolve and adapt.
3. You gain more insight and experience.
4. New avenues open up for you.

Certain decisions are made with the intent to weather them out, to make them endure *whatever* the changes that happen to us. Decisions involving marriage, career, and religious affiliation all typically are made for such long hauls. The value of maintaining stability outweighs the few gains that could be had by constantly switching. There is great value to this kind of stability. Yet, even this resolve does not save us from the need to address change.

Decisions also involve uncertainty. We live—and decide—in a world where we rarely know precisely what events will happen and what the exact consequences of our actions will be. If you knew all outcomes for sure, deciding would be a snap.

Uncertainty complicates the decision-making process because it says that some factors determining the outcome are partially out of our sight or control. For example, for the average person on the street, the stock market is a very risky game. Precise knowledge of the trends and forthcoming mergers is closely held. Even for a stockbroker, this information is not sufficient, for there are major uncertainties in the way the market will react to political events, international conflicts, and fluctuations in the economy.

> **If you knew all the outcomes for sure, deciding would be a snap.**

Scientific decision makers have developed quantitative methods to handle uncertainty. It's important to understand, however, that these methods do not *eliminate* uncertainty. Instead, they *assess* the potential effect of the uncertainties on the outcomes. Sensitivity studies allow scientific decision makers to understand how sensitive the outcome is to small changes (uncertainties) in the input. Then they consider how probable those uncertainties are, and work toward choices that leave them with a better known level of risk or vulnerability. Usually, they are not in a position to do anything about the uncertainty itself other than gauge its effect. In other words, they are making *educated* guesses.

The conclusion that I draw about change and uncertainty in decision making is this: *Don't try to eliminate change and uncertainty; learn to live with them.* To do this, always monitor your decisions. Keep track of important changes and ask yourself if your present responses are still adequate. Stay in constant contact with your environment to make sure that you see coming trends.

Even after you've made a good decision, the elements of change and uncertainty may cause you to refine it further. This is not cause for alarm or skepticism. By acknowledging uncertainty and change, you will find it easier to navigate around them. Monitoring your decisions does not mean that you must always sway with the breeze, only that you resolve to correct the vessel's course when necessary.

INOCULATE YOURSELF AGAINST ANXIETY

Anxiety (once again!) In Chapter 1, we mentioned that anxiety is a useful messenger. Sometimes, though, after the message has been delivered, the messenger hangs around and makes a nuisance of itself. In this section, we shall consider some ways anxiety can be reduced *after* the decision has been made.

Learning to deal with anxiety is a life skill, not just a decision skill. For some people, even deciding to buy a new suit can cause great anxiety if it elicits long-standing fears about their appearance, practicality, frugality, or self-worth.

Postdecisional anxiety occurs especially in decisions requiring major trade-offs. Whenever you think about the forgone
advantages, there are feelings of regret, loss, and deprivation.
You feel, "Surely there must have been some way to pursue this
path without having had to give up all those other advantages."
The first time a major setback is experienced, such thoughts run
rampant.

Anxiety is a nuisance because it multiplies the size of the
threat or challenge in your mind's eye. The person suffering
anxiety doesn't have a good sense for how big the threat is and
whether they are capable of handling it. The first step is similar
to the way we handled obstacles in Chapter 5. You must see the
potential threat in greater detail to realize that you have many
options. You don't have to accept the very worst option that
your imagination can summon.

Anxiety is intimately related to perception, attention, and
imagination. Think of anxiety as a disorder of the imagination.
We all project the effect of our possible actions into the future,
so as to be able to pick those that are of greatest benefit. Anxious
people do not see the future in realistic terms. Instead, their
imagination projects a horror movie in which they are the prin-
cipal victims.

The anxious person is hypervigilant. He or she spends too
much energy watching for disasters that never happen. Knowing
this fact is not much help to the person suffering from anxiety.
He or she feels that when things are going well, it means that
he or she has no problems. This is simply wrong; everyone who
lives has problems. They are part of life itself. The person who
has conquered anxiety realizes that things are going well when
he or she is *equal* to his or her problems, when he or she does
not feel overwhelmed by them or flinch in their face.

Finally, the anxious person is too sensitive to pain. The
reason that he or she is so watchful for disaster in the first place
is that he or she is extraordinarily affected by the experience of
feeling hurt, be it in the form of loneliness, suffering, loss,
disappointment, frustration, or rejection. Often in the childhood
of the anxiety-prone person, there was considerable deprivation
or lack of parental sensitivity to the child's needs, emotional
well-being, or recovery from physical illness.

> ## The anxious person spends too much energy watching for disasters that never happen.

If anxiety is preventing you from becoming an effective decision maker, you need to apply corrective techniques. If you don't know how to control anxiety, it will come back day after day, even after you have made your "final" decision and committed yourself to a course of action.

Overcome anxiety by facing it directly. If you try to ignore the negatives causing you to be anxious, they will multiply like weeds on a lawn. The only way to be rid of them is by directly confronting them and pulling them up by the roots. Don't give them a chance to multiply. As each anxiety cue arises, find out why it sets off a catastrophic reaction—and question its validity right on the spot.

HOW TO BREAK OUT OF AN ANXIETY LOOP

The phrase "anxiety loop" refers to a major characteristic of anxiety: It keeps its victims going around in little circles, getting nowhere fast. As soon as the anxious person defines the problem and poses solutions, he or she rejects the solutions that he or she has just proposed. The anxious person feels helpless, because he or she *wants* to escape the trap, but can't find the exit. Here are some techniques that may help:

1. Acknowledge your anxiety. By recognizing and accepting your anxiety, you'll find it easier to change. By openly admitting your anxiety, you will be in a better position to reduce the shame of potentially exhibiting it in front of others and looking foolish. When you can identify that anxiety is a problem for you, you can read books, talk to friends, or seek professional help to overcome it. You'll be able to benefit from the knowledge that others in a similar situation have overcome anxiety, and that you can do the same. You'll begin to believe in your own ability to overcome anxiety.

2. Talk your situation over with others who are supportive. Listen to see whether you are catastrophizing. Solicit their advice about what to do.

3. Don't demand so much of yourself. Be patient with yourself. Learn to adjust your expectations. Discount the advice of people who are motivated (for one reason or another) to feed you unrealistic expectations. Don't insist that you should be able to make a *single* clever move that extracts you from a bad situation. Don't even demand that you should be able to *understand* what your whole problem is instantly. It takes time to understand any complex and worthwhile situation. The demand that you instantly see through it all is a form of self-punishment.

   Do not engage in a self-hate campaign. Yes, maybe you made a mistake or displayed poor judgment. Or, perhaps, fate has dealt you a bitter blow. But these events do not diminish your value as a person. You have an obligation to respect yourself, even if others are disappointed in you or your actions.

4. State the realistic outcomes of your alternatives. Describe how you would feel if these realistic outcomes materialized instead of the worst case ones. Correct distortions in your assessment of the situation.

5. Understand the mechanics of your anxiety. Learn what its cues are and which situations bring it on. When you feel confident with this knowledge, try to *interrupt* the anxiety process when you feel it coming on. Distract yourself from it, trick yourself into ignoring it, get a friend to coach you through it, do whatever it takes to upset its automatic action.

6. *Do* something, however small, that is one step in the right direction for you. Gain evidence about your ability to handle things rather than speculate about them.

7. Emotionally inoculate yourself against anxiety. *Prepare* yourself for the negatives. Rehearse for better performance. Deliberately deal with the negatives in measured form before they hit you with full strength. Test out your storm anchors in a gale wind, not in a hurricane of devastating force. The confidence that you can handle the preparation will help place the larger challenge in perspective.

8. Don't lose hope. This may sound preachy, but many people find that when a black cloud blows over, much can be salvaged—met-

aphorically, if not literally. Read inspirational stories that emphasize man's ability to bounce back after abject failure, to recover from "terminal" illnesses, and to overcome "insurmountable" difficulties.[1]

9. Spend time specifically set aside for relaxation and renewal. For an hour a day, find something that absorbs you so thoroughly that you forget the "problem."

10. Develop greater frustration tolerance. Learn that a certain amount of pain or discomfort will not ruin you or make you unlovable.

11. Be kind to yourself. Don't punish yourself for having anxious thoughts or recognizing that your anxiety has hindered you in the past. Do not deprive yourself of essential everyday needs (or a few luxuries!) in an effort to prepare for a disaster that may never come.

Don't get carried away with "insurance policy thinking," in which all effort and energy is exclusively taken up with preparing and planning for emergencies and disasters. Instead, take active steps to further your goals *in spite of* the potential disasters.

Anxiety becomes more bearable by moderating your expectations. It's natural to have high hopes when you start a marriage, job, project, or hobby. If these hopes aren't realized as quickly as you want, anxiety may set in. You may begin to doubt yourself: Are you equal to the challenge? Did you set your goals too high? Were you deluding yourself? Can you afford to continue? For what length of time should the experiment be conducted before the evidence is gathered and inferences drawn?

Similar questions occur to those considering becoming consultants. In my book on the consulting business,[2] I discussed their most frequently asked question: How many years must you be a consultant before you are considered "successful"? I know now that this is a trick question. The

---

[1] For a readable and compassionate treatment of how to bounce back from failure, see *When Smart People Fail* by Carole Hyatt and Linda Gottlieb (1987). The authors give almost two hundred examples of how people survived failure, reinterpreted it, and then used its positive elements to emerge stronger and more successful.

[2] *Inside the Technical Consulting Business* (1986).

measure of success is not, "How long" but instead, "Are you doing what you want to do right now? Does your step-by-step progress make you happy?"

Another good way to handle doubt is to make sure there are some immediate benefits from your decision. Acknowledge the progress you are making. Celebrate your victories, however small. Share your benefits with others. Work at things you really believe in, things that can nourish you.

Finally, the paralysis and stress of anxiety can be relieved by developing a sense of humor. More than anything else, humor helps us gain perspective. With humor, we experience the over-seriousness that we give to our problems. Humor makes us aware of our pretensions, our foibles, our unrealistic expectations—in a way that serious analysis simply cannot.

WHAT TO DO IN A CRISIS

If you are in a crisis situation, it will probably take time and planning to extract yourself *gracefully*. Survival does not allow elegant solutions. If the situation allows you no recourse but to act quickly, you must resign yourself to a certain amount of suffering or loss. Nevertheless, here are a few rules of thumb that may help you minimize the potentially damaging effects of a crisis:

- Decide one thing at a time; don't attempt to rearrange all aspects of your life in the middle of an emergency.

- Accept what has happened; don't spend all your energy trying to deny it.

- Do not be afraid to ask friends for help, resources, and contacts.

- Pay close consideration to the people you are trading with. Especially in resolving employment, financial, and romantic crises, don't look just at the carrot dangling in front of you, but also at the person who dangles it. Do they keep their word? Are they ethical? What are their motives for the trade?

- Attend to major details first.

- Keep plans simple; don't innovate in a panic.

- Buy more time.

- Try to make your decisions reversible.

- Parallel-path your options; pursue more than one option at the same time to increase the probability of a useful outcome.

- Never give up a major goal when you're feeling down.

- Trust the power of your own observations. Especially in a rapidly changing environment, authoritative or quantitative information is generally useless. It's probably outdated. If the crisis is widespread, expect some *dis*information from those who are motivated to manipulate people in your situation.

In most crisis situations, expect to lighten your baggage somehow. Certain of your luxuries, obligations, and activities—that you have previously considered inviolate—may need to be temporarily dropped. In particular, don't feel that you absolutely must honor commitments that were based on conditions that no longer exist. Recognizing that you are in a crisis means you acknowledge that radical measures must be taken, that you are sounding the alarm. Crises demand that you use a new set of criteria that is not based on optimizing your situation.

In a true emergency, save yourself by whatever means you can ("any port in a storm"). Therefore, crisis decision making is inherently tactical. Use *any* method that works to survive the crisis. However, when the crisis is over, you should salvage what remains and reformulate long-range plans. Don't naively hope that a crisis maneuver painlessly leads to valid long-term solutions. Trying to convert a crisis solution into a long-term one is usually inappropriate, because the criteria for the two will necessarily be different. Converting a crisis solution into a long-term one is like riding around on a spare tire designed for emergency use only. It leads to problems all its own.

Everybody has crises occasionally, but some people are *crisis prone*. One crisis after another just seems to happen. However, upon closer inspection, it becomes clear that these people *invite* their crises into their lives unwittingly. They neglect essential chores required to keep their lives working smoothly. They "seize the day" (which is not bad in itself) without regard for obligations that cannot be put off.

Want to have a crisis with your car? It's easy. Just

- Neglect to replace the tires when they are worn
- Be too busy to add oil
- Load up with three or four drinks before you drive
- Tailgate frequently
- Fail to have your brakes checked regularly

While being overcautious leads to unnecessary maintenance costs, the other extreme—total lack of caution—is more common. My experience in consulting is that 80 percent of all business crises could be prevented by only moderate foresight and concern.

Constant crises are a sign of internal disorder. They indicate a personality deficit or an unconscious wish to defeat one's own efforts. Well-balanced people need a certain amount of order in their lives and try to minimize crisis decisions. Crisis decision making may be necessary at times, but it is a severely limiting form of action. It usually leads nowhere and improves nothing. A crisis decision buys only a few days, weeks, or months before it requires another temporary patch. Effective decision makers avoid letting crises determine the direction of their life. They do not substitute crisis management for strategic planning.

> ## Crisis management is not a substitute for strategic planning!

Finally, not all crises lead to negative results. Very often, a crisis brings many opportunities with it that would not otherwise become available. Seize the worthwhile opportunities arising in this manner and use them as a source of personal growth.

REDEFINE FAILURE

The secret to redefining failure is separating your self-esteem from the results of your "experiments." If a relationship or job doesn't work out, it's easy to conclude that *you* aren't right, that the resulting failure means that *you* failed. But the experimenter is not the experiment! Do not make the error of associating your self with the outcome.

Experiments with negative outcomes are valid. They tell you that you need to regroup and try the experiment in a different way or under different conditions. Perhaps you need to try a *different* experiment. In all cases, negative results don't relieve you of the need to continue experimenting until you get successful results.

> Thomas Edison's search for the electric light bulb is a wonderful example of how failure does not stop a persistent person. Edison first tried forming filaments from twelve different metals. No luck. He then tried carbonizing forty-nine carbonaceous materials in an attempt to produce a material that could withstand the high temperatures. No luck. On his fiftieth try, in 1879, he discovered that carbonized paper, which formed a long homogeneous fiber, worked reasonably well.
>
> Yet, bulb life was still short. In 1880, Edison found that carbonized bamboo improved the bulb's longevity. In 1893, he advanced to squirted cellulose filament. In 1906, he switched to tantalum wire. In 1907, he finally arrived at tungsten wire, which is still used in modern incandescent bulbs.
>
> In all, Edison's invention of the light bulb took 9,000 failures to get to 1 success. Edison, the world's most prolific inventor (with 1,093 patents) also had more failures than any other inventor!

By semantically qualifying your experiments, you can allow yourself to risk again. To do this, state the *conditions* under which you carried out the experiments. Suppose you're learning how to do a figure-skating jump. You try it ten times and fall ten times. You might conclude that you can't do that jump—period. In qualifying the experiment semantically, you would also note that perhaps you made the attempts with dull skates that didn't grip the ice properly. Or perhaps in all ten attempts, your arms were in the wrong position and worked against completing the jump. If you tried the experiment with sharp skates or some tips on arm position, the results might be very different!

Emotionally, we tend to drop off semantic qualification. Instead, we focus solely on our helpless feeling of losing and being vulnerable. Part of the answer is learning how to contain these negative emotions while you conduct an intelligent search for ways to modify the experiment.

The experimenter is not the experiment!

Failure can be overcome through a four-step *emotional training course*:

1. Redefine it.
2. Qualify it semantically.
3. Learn from it.
4. Consider it vital information for your next try.

Failed experiments often have enormous *salvage value.* They can be restructured by focusing on the partial victories contained within. We usually fail to acknowledge such positives within a failed experiment, because the bad feelings associated with the overall outcome cloud our vision. In this way, we deprive ourselves of up to 90 percent of our own useful experience!

To restructure a failed experiment more effectively, list both the mistakes and the victories contained within it. What lessons have you learned from the results? Can you make any resolutions for more effective experiments in the future? Can you intuitively say what aspects could be changed to improve the results? Is there a way to make a new effort that uses the winning elements and shuns the negative ones?

An important aspect of transcending failure is *giving ourselves permission to fail.* Most of us have been taught as children that failing is terrible, that it must be avoided like the plague. We intuitively learn that failing reduces your worth as a human being. Nothing could be farther from the truth. The only person who doesn't fail is the corpse buried six feet under. For the rest of us, living means we must experience failure.

The biggest gift you can give yourself, your children, and your friends is the permission to fail. You—and your loved ones—need permission to take chances without the penalty of being censured for the outcome ("I told you so").

Learning how to survive defeat makes you a stronger and more resourceful person. When you are able to accept failure as an inseparable part of life, you'll be more willing to reach out for the things you want. You'll feel comfortable in allowing yourself an "error margin" in your plans that specifically acknowledges the inevitable fumbles, misunderstandings, and inefficiencies that are part of any new venture.

I am not a proponent of the "school of hard knocks." It is my observation that failures, in themselves, do not make a person strong. Strength comes, instead, from knowing experientially that failures will neither destroy nor deter you in the long run. Real growth comes from experiencing yourself as powerful enough to achieve the positives in spite of the negatives.

AVOID "GOAL VACUUM" BY ACKNOWLEDGING LOSSES

Sudden loss of a valued job, marriage partner, limb, money, friendship, or opportunity—can have a disorienting and paralyzing effect. When an actively pursued goal breaks apart or becomes impossible, many people experience a phenomenon I call *goal vacuum*. Individuals in its grasp notice a sense of confusion. They know they have to make new choices, but all new goals appear undesirable. None can fill the void left by the disappearance of the old. The emotional energy has nowhere to go.

There is no magic solution to this problem. The loss must be grieved and ultimately overcome. Like all grieving processes, there are stages: first shock, then disbelief, later anger, eventually acceptance, and finally recovery. It's important to understand the unreasonableness of expecting any new situation to fill the shoes of the old situation quickly. Every new situation requires building from the ground up. The new risks and compromises—as well as rewards—are never strictly commensurate with the old. The flow of emotional energy to the new situation must be moderated to avoid displacing the old emotional flow full strength onto it.

Gradual losses are often more insidious than sudden ones. There's no single identifiable event that announces them, yet the goal vacuum is just as real. All that is noticed at first, again, is the sense of confusion—not knowing what step to take next.

One perceives changes on the horizon and tries to figure out whether they are real or mirages. Because there is no sudden shock, this doubt (the stage of disbelief) persists for an extended period.

The situation is analogous to that of a person gradually becoming aware that they are caught in a massive forest fire. As they move forward, they perceive that they are heading toward a fire. They look behind, and, to their horror, discover that the fire is forming there also. There seems to be no simple way out.

People have difficulty steering a clear course in the midst of a forest fire because the extreme situation demands too much of their energy and attention. Having a strong sense of direction is one thing that can stabilize a person in such an environment. Without a goal constantly in sight and constantly affirmed, foggy vision induces them to walk around in circles.

Later in the grieving cycle, one becomes angry with oneself for having made errors in judgment. It's easy to displace this anger onto others or the "system" for being so intractable and unreceptive. It takes time before this anger subsides and things can be accepted the way they are. When that happens, one is ready to make new choices that reflect the adaptive learning. As suggested, these new choices may not possess, at first, the same emotional intensity as the old, but they are more likely to be satisfying in the future.

Learning to accept a loss by acknowledging it, feeling its pain, mourning it, and then moving on—is often the most direct path to winning. If you feel that a loss damages your self-esteem or proves that you are undesirable or unlovable, you're blackmailing yourself into either denying your losses or falsely advertising them as victories. This can be done only at the expense of denying your emotional responses and pretending—even to yourself—that things are okay.

Being able to accept your losses on an emotional level is the key to moving on. If you refuse to acknowledge important losses, you'll always be looking over your shoulder for that old situation to reappear magically. With your gaze fixed on past benefits, you'll never be able to commit fully to the new.

A wonderful sense of clarity arises when you have fully accepted the compromises, risks, partial failures, and regrets inherent in a chosen course of action. As feelings of confusion subside, you'll be more able to commit your energies to the activities and relationships you choose.

Learning how to accept a loss is an important part of winning.

WHEN SHOULD YOU REVERSE A DECISION?

After having committed to a course of action, running into a major obstacle may force you to reexamine your decision. The conditions on which you based your previous choice may now differ significantly. Do these changes affect the goal itself or merely the path you use to get there?

At some point, of course, insurmountable obstacles or unacceptable losses will require abandoning the goal and finding a new course of action. Short of that point, you'll need to determine the additional resources you're willing to risk in order to continue and the changes in approach that may be required.

The obstacles or losses causing concern may be sudden or gradual. Sometimes, a single poignant event is all it takes to make us see the emotional reality of a situation. More often than not, the changes are gradual, and we must evaluate subtle, but long-established trends.

Consider, for example, the marriage or job that was originally paying good benefits and that has gradually gone downhill. Now, it seems that the benefits are gone, leaving only the liabilities. Recently, both parties take each other's presence for granted. At what point is this arrangement no longer worthwhile?

One major factor in considering such a decision reversal is the *investment* in your present course of action. To assess your response, ask yourself:

1. How much is at risk?

2. How much will it "cost" to maintain your present course?

3. Are you willing to accept that extra cost or effort? Or is it time to cut your losses?

4. What other alternatives are available to you? How much do they cost?

Sound judgment is essential in assessing item 2 correctly. When the cost or effort starts to increase, there's often not enough data to ascertain whether it will abate or escalate without bounds. Especially in competitive situations, *escalation*[3] can get out of hand. It's human nature to misperceive your real position in a competitive situation and tell yourself, "Just a little bit more and I'll win." The belief that you're very close to the goal—and have too much invested to lose—leads to staying in the game longer than you should. By not setting limits on your involvement, you can fool yourself and suffer losses far greater than you can afford.

Realistic perception of the obstacle is necessary before you can develop a good response to decision reversal. (Chapter 5 gave a few methods for that.) Once you see the situation clearly, you can choose from four general strategies:

SWITCH: Abandon the situation and choose anew. This means that you must openly acknowledge that the situation is untenable. Switching is frequently the correct thing to do, but it can be a bitter pill to swallow. You may hesitate even when it is clear that you *must* abandon. First, it means you have to admit your losses. Second, it means that you have to admit limitations on your resources. Even if the obstacle can be overcome, the price required to continue may be higher than you are willing to pay. Recognizing these limitations is painful. You cannot be

---

[3] See Max H. Bazerman, *Judgment in Managerial Decision Making* (New York: John Wiley & Sons, 1986), pp. 68–80, for an interesting and readable discussion of the factors affecting the tendency to escalate. Bazerman suggests numerous ways to avoid escalation: Set limits on your commitment in advance, don't use the escalating behavior of other people to justify your own, actively determine why you are continuing on a path that has significant losses, closely monitor the costs involved, and remain vigilant for the telltale signs of escalation.

anything, or have everything, you wish. Each of us has obstacles that—for all practical purposes—are insurmountable.

Reversing a decision makes many people uncomfortable. They fear it makes them appear inconsistent.[4] They now have to announce that their course of action has changed. They worry that others may resist the new course—or worse—gloat at the news and take it as an announcement that they have made a mistake. Others may blast them with the proverbial "I told you so's."

People in the merchandising field take advantage of this psychological tendency. Knowing how loath many people are to reverse decisions (purchasing decisions in particular), they offer money-back guarantees. Cunning merchandisers fully understand that a sizable percentage of customers will not return an item, even when it is clearly defective or broken! Customers reluctant to take up a money-back guarantee are usually too sensitive to the imagined shame of having to reverse their decision.

ANTE UP: Pay the increased costs or meet the requirement for increased effort and commitment. When your investment in a course of action is very high, this may prove an effective way of maintaining your advantages. Others, who have less to gain by paying the increased price, will drop out of contention. If you are pursuing this strategy, learning coping skills will help you accommodate the increased cost-benefit ratio.

FIGHT: Actively resist the demand for increased cost or effort. Often, the other side will back down or otherwise adapt to your requests, leaving you with the original cost-benefit ratio. Of course, waging a resistance campaign has a cost of its own, so this option still embraces an escalation of sorts.

HEDGE: Split your options into two or more parallel paths. This insurance policy approach allows you to investigate the merits of other options before you commit fully to them. It also warns others that you intend to limit the amount of escalation you will tolerate. The danger in hedging is that you may not have sufficient energy or resources to carry it out.

---

[4] Of course, if you reverse too many decisions, your credibility goes down. Others will shy away from you if *nothing* remains consistent.

ON REVERSING DECISIONS

- Typically, one out of four decisions is reversed.

- Reverse sooner rather than later.

- Fifty percent of all reversals are due to discovering hidden aspects of the deal. To minimize reversals, therefore, investigate all important aspects before making a commitment.

- Before reversing, make sure you can give good reasons for doing it. To maintain credibility, you must be able to defend the reversal as a rational act.

- Maintain hopeless situations only if you like punishing yourself.

- Reversing carries a price. Not reversing also carries a price. Take your pick.

- One year after a reversal, nobody cares. A few may remember, but life goes on.

GOOD DECISION MAKING IS ADAPTIVE

The issue of reversal highlights an important psychological aspect of decisions: Good decision making is adaptive. It adjusts to environmental changes as you pursue your goals. Reluctance to adapt is due to three major factors:

1. You have to learn new techniques. Most people regard such effort as time taken away from the really important thing, the "substance." They need to develop a more holistic attitude about this; without adaptive change, nothing happens!

Meet new problems with new solutions. Often, the old solutions are simply not adequate to the situation. The new problem may demand finding new tools to forge an adequate response. Knowing when to discard old solutions is never completely obvious. No one will hang a sign out for you that says, "Stop that old routine; it doesn't work." Instead, you must become sensitive to how the environment is changing, and to how well your existing set of tools and responses are working. Remember, the measure is not how expert you are in performing a particular set of actions or how much you like to use a certain solution, but how well the solution works.

Meet new problems with new solutions.

---

2. You have to acknowledge your losses. The fact that you made mistakes or suffered setbacks can reflect poorly on your public image. In a competitive and gossip-prone world, people who have little self-esteem of their own may feel elevated by your misfortunes and gloat at your losses. If you have poor tolerance for such wounds to your self-esteem, it may be easier to abandon a project than to admit temporary defeat. The deficiency of this strategy is that you never reach the goals you truly desire.

3. You have to reaffirm your goals in the face of newly discovered resistance. People who approved of your prior actions may not approve of the new actions needed to overcome the obstacle. Or you may discover that the cost of pursuing the goal is higher than you initially estimated. Or you may encounter conditions less ideal than anticipated. In all these situations, you will find yourself reluctant to adapt if you do not have a strong sense of self-esteem. Chapter 11 offers guidelines and suggestions to help access this stronger and more confident "you."

11

AFFIRM YOUR DECISIONS, AFFIRM YOURSELF

LEARN TO TRUST YOURSELF

Many people, when faced with an unacceptable situation, constantly ask themselves, "Am I sure of what I'm seeing here?" They question their ability to see things correctly rather than accept the meaning of the situation. Often, the negative situation is one in which they are being hurt or compromised. Constant rechecking ("Am I sure?") is the perfect *interruption* to the process of perception. In this way, the stress of accepting the challenge is avoided.

People with obsessive personalities fall into this trap. Their demand for orderliness serves them well in many aspects of life.

It gives them, among other benefits, a great deal of control. But when it comes to admitting a *dis*-ordering perception, obsessives resort to constant rechecking. Their *orderliness* (translate: desire for no change or highly structured change at best) limits their ability to make decisions that require risk (translate: unstructured change).

LEARNING TO TRUST YOURSELF IS

- Allowing yourself to make decisions

- Allowing yourself to change

- Permitting yourself to take risks

- Discovering that losing will not annihilate you

- Letting go of the need to control everything

- Relying on your innate resources

- Trusting your own perceptions

- Not rechecking constantly to be "absolutely sure"

A sense of trust in yourself and your own worth is essential to good decision making. This basic trust *precedes* the decision-making process. You either feel worthy or not, but it's not something that you rationally determine. Trying to "decide" if you're worthy is the ultimate procrastination, because the process can never be completed.

This chapter shows how to overcome some of the psychological mechanisms that can undermine self-trust. The last section, on affirmations, suggests ways to access and enhance feelings that can lead you to greater self-trust.

> **Trying to "decide" if you're worthy is the ultimate procrastination.**

DECIDE WHO DECIDES

> . . . I discover that I have no means of self-affirmation
> other than my acts themselves. "I" am . . . the subject
> pole of my acts.
>
> [In deciding,] I implicate myself in the project, the
> anticipated action is "to be done by me."
>
> —Paul Ricoeur, *Freedom and Nature* (1966)

Many people look at decision making solely as an intellectual exercise in problem solving. They think that decisions can be detached from the person making them. In almost all cases, nothing could be farther from the truth. As Paul Ricoeur emphasizes in his phenomenological study of decision making, the decision maker imputes himself into the situation by taking the actions indicated by his will.

A decision maker cannot withhold his or her self from the process without rendering the decision maladaptive or ineffective. If the self that must take action is underdeveloped, insecure, or uncertain, the resulting decision-making process will be flawed. To understand why this is so, let's briefly digress into the field of self-psychology.

Failure is an assault on the ego. If your ego is healthy and strong, you can withstand major failures without undermining your sense of identity. A weak ego, on the other hand, is threatened by small and even insignificant failures.

People with weak egos have—unbeknown to themselves—a poor sense of judgment. They will not be able to differentiate between various opportunities carefully enough. More specifically, they have difficulty judging the suitability of a situation *relative to their own needs and goals*. This problem is not external, but internal: Their egos lack detailed structure. Stated more simply, they can't say who they are.

If you can't say, *in detail,* who you are and what you value, you'll have difficulty *assessing* situations and opportunities to see if they can meet your needs. Further, since most situations also involve meeting the needs or requirements of others, you may also lack the ability to know to what degree you should adapt to their needs without totally compromising your own.

This meshing of needs is never a black-and-white issue. It's not a matter of finding the situation that perfectly matches your needs A, B, C with corresponding needs A, B, C from others. The issue is gray instead: Can you find a "good enough" match of your needs A, B, C with the corresponding needs X, Y, Z of others?

People with weak egos have— unbeknown to themselves—a poor sense of judgment.

A person with a weak ego sees the many shades of gray, but then distills them into a single black-and-white question: "Am I being accepted or rejected?" The poorly developed psychological defenses do a great job of protecting the ego against the pain of rejection, but do not, at the same time, allow sufficient information by which to make useful judgments.

People with weak egos give up the power of choice in their own lives. In work, their company chooses them. In romance, their partner chooses them. In social activities, they go where they are most warmly received, no matter whether that's where they *want* to be.

Effective decision makers tend to actualize their values and goals through their decisions. Interestingly, the ability to make good decisions does not depend on *what* those particular values and goals are. Adolf Hitler had values that most of us would not support, but there is little doubt that he was an effective decision maker. Decision-making ability is distinctly different from the *content* of the underlying ethical judgments and values.

The ultimate measure of decisions is not their rationality, but whether they help you become what you want to be, whether they elicit the results you desire. Thus, the quality of a decision is largely subjective; no one can say for sure what *you* want. Even in large groups and corporations, decision quality is never an objective fact. There is rarely uniform consensus on what the emerging group identity should be.

SET BOUNDARIES TO YOUR IDENTITY

The weakly structured ego does not have a firm sense of "who I am" and "who I am not." The self is too plastic to assert itself or actively fight for its place in the sun. Instead, when resistance is met, the weak ego withdraws or changes its sense of self rather than meet the resistance head on.

As your personal identity crystallizes, you will feel more comfortable choosing. You'll be able to attain your goals by means that are consistent with your self-image. Your means will reflect the individual background, strengths, talents, and preferences that you bring to the situation.

Individuals who do not have a strong sense of identity may have definite goals regarding income, love, friendship, community, and so on, but are often unable to choose *reasonable* means to realize them. They are too anxious to achieve the end without looking carefully enough to see if the means are compatible with their self. Typically, they prematurely switch means, use inappropriate means, or hold on to outdated means long after they have ceased to be helpful. A weak identity leads to using methods that conflict with personal values.

People who lack a strong sense of identity often boast that they have many, many possibilities open to them. Yet, a superabundance of options works against their best interest. It encourages experimenting with options that are clearly inappropriate. Indeed, the person who is undefined, unlabeled, aloof, and unaffiliated does retain more possibilities. In this superficial sense, they are powerful and free. But, at a deeper level, they're submerged by their possibilities. Their life is deprived of the nourishment that can only be provided by choices, commitment, and relatedness.

As soon as you choose, you're thrust out of the world of possibility—where you can be all things to all people—and into the finite world of relationship, where one choice necessarily precludes others. Making that choice not only produces benefits, but also requires liabilities and commitment.

If the ego is not strong enough to protect itself from the resistance encountered in relationship, it will find ways to withdraw and hide. One such way is unconsciously to make safety into a higher priority than growth by remaining preoccupied with possibilities.

One exercise that helps overcome a fragile ego is to assert and affirm who you are—and just as importantly—who you are *not*. When making decisions in specific contexts, it's useful to write a list. For example, in a work context, one man wrote:

WHO I AM

I am a person who

- Sees people regularly
- Has his own office
- Helps others
- Does creative things
- Does writing and research
- Uses psychological concepts

WHO I AM NOT

I am not a person who

- Sells merchandise
- Does manual labor
- Travels extensively for work
- Works for radical political groups
- Likes banking and investment work
- Argues legal points

STRUCTURE RISKS SO AS TO DEVELOP CONFIDENCE

The field of *object relations psychology* deals with emotional disorders that arise in the first few years of life. These disorders persist—almost invisibly—through adolescence and adulthood.[1] I mention this specialized field here because it sheds light on several faulty decision processes that occur in adult life.

---

[1] See N. Gregory Hamilton, *Self and Others* (1988), for a lucid and up-to-date survey of this fascinating area of psychology.

According to the object relations view, the child who grows up with mothering that's not quite "good enough" develops an invisible split in its personality. From an early age, there are two Johnnies. One is visible from the outside and obeys all the rules. He valiantly tries to gain attention by becoming special, brilliant, handsome, or talented. The other Johnny is almost invisible. He's a hungry and neglected child who remains emotionally arrested at the age of two. He tends to perceive the world only in black-and-white terms. He can't articulate his quandary in adult language when he is two, and he *remains* unable to articulate it even as an adult.

According to psychologist D. W. Winnicott, most mothers are, in fact, "good enough." They provide sufficient loving, soothing, touching, caressing, and mirroring to make their infant know—on a preverbal level—that it's valued and worthy. In instances where the mothering is severely deficient, the infant's emotional development is adversely affected. The infant learns (again, preverbally) that it's *not* worthy of love just because it exists. The infant develops the idea that it must do something *special* to deserve the love that has been withheld. Furthermore, if the infant receives attention for those special performances, it mistakes that applause for love.

Object relations therapy accesses the two-year-old within and allows him or her to resume emotional growth. This occurs in two phases. First, the person is given enough empathic nurturing by the therapist to tentatively relax the defenses protecting the helpless infant within. Once these defenses have been reduced, Johnny (the adult) will be able to see—for the first time— that there is a helpless infant within who needs to grow up. In fact, that helpless infant wants to grow up, but is fearful of the dangers such growth poses to his fragile self.

The infant within must be shown, gradually and skillfully, that he can negotiate resistance in the external world in terms that are not black and white. In particular, the infant within learns that committing to a person or group (that is, forming an object relation) does not necessarily imply annihilation of his self or total control by the other.

Erik Erickson, in his study of emotional development, showed that at this level, the issues are:

trust *versus* mistrust

autonomy *versus* shame

The emerging self learns to steady itself and integrate an initiative (*act*) in the midst of gray situations. In the language of object relations psychology, the self learns *object constancy:* Some people can be trusted and relied upon, even if they *temporarily* resist, disagree, or leave. The glue underlying object constancy is the unconditional love remembered from the infant's preverbal experience of being nurtured.

Nobody can go back and undo the past. But adults can undergo present experiences that simulate the childhood situation *psychologically*. These experiences provide a second chance to replace the deficient learning. The transference situation in psychoanalysis is exactly one such controlled environment. Emotional growth resumes by exposing the child within to situations similar to the ones that caused splitting of the self. Only this time, the child within is guided to take the leap of courage. With proper therapeutic nurture, the emerging self learns

- How to act in spite of its fears
- How to face external resistance rather than withdraw from it
- How to release the need to always be in control
- How to state its needs without feeling that it is attacking the other person or group (the object)
- How to refuse the object's demands without undue worry that it will be abandoned

Learning these shades of gray does not come cheaply. The person with an obsessive personality or narcissistic deficit resulting from inadequate mothering is ultrasensitive to the defeats that are necessary to discover the conditions under which trust is justified. Such people are quick to point out that there are circumstances in which just one mistake, just one demand, or just one affront—will cause the other person to leave forever. They overlook and discount exactly those situations in which demonstrated mutuality, elasticity, and forgiveness make abundantly clear an underlying desire to maintain relationship.

Until the two-year-old within is gently encouraged to make these experiments, his defenses will prevent him from progressing in these emotional directions. What he will learn instead is to become self-sufficient. He will withdraw in "splendid isola-tion" to enact his grandiose fantasy. He places himself in the situation of never having to face the confrontation he fears he is unable to handle. Contained in this fashion, aggressive energies have nowhere to go but inward. As a result, in many instances Johnny becomes masochistic. He can't seem to avoid undermin-ing his own efforts.

The narcissistic tendency is to withdraw and gather up all energies within oneself. At all costs, confronting another is avoided, anger is avoided, depending on another is avoided. The two-year-old within plays with himself. He's unable to form meaningful relationships because he has avoided an essential social relationship skill: He cannot assert himself in a resisting environment (that is, in the real world!). In other words, his "self" is so shaky that it cannot bear to be asserted. If he asserts himself, the all-or-nothing fear of "annihilate versus be annihi-lated" overwhelms his capacity to cope. If he lets go of his death grip on the anger valve, he may not be able to control it within socially acceptable limits.

What do I mean when I say that a person's ego structure is undeveloped and shaky? The two-year-old within has not ad-equately experienced his *self* in relation to others in a dyadic (face-to-face) fashion. When he pushes, he has neither a firm sense of his own strength nor the perceptual tools by which to measure his effect on others. He has difficulty maintaining equi-librium within a relationship: First he pushes too hard, then too weakly. It's like the first time a driving student uses a manual shift car. In trying to find the friction point of the clutch, first she lets it out too much, then not enough. After an hour of stalls and tire chirps, she learns just how much is enough for various road conditions and engine speeds.

The undeveloped self has not learned how to deal effectively with resistance. It's not sufficiently sure of its own identity to know when to say "No." Neither does it feel comfortable in exercising autonomous action (saying "Yes"). Instead, it's overly dependent on the object (person or group) for validation and approval. ("If they reject me, I don't count; maybe I don't even exist!")

Because the undeveloped self always looks over its shoulder for a parent who is no longer there, it has great difficulty making decisions. The "I" that would impute itself into the situation is *emotionally* overwhelmed.

Ironically, this emotional inadequacy can exist side by side with outstanding competence in performing the *intellectual* deliberations that partially support every decision. Nevertheless, intellectual brilliance can never totally compensate for inadequate emotional resources. The hidden emotional mandates eventually undermine or override the solutions posed by the intellect.

These decision problems gradually disappear as the self becomes strong enough to tolerate a higher level of uncertainty, criticism, and sacrifice. Aggressive energies become rechanneled from the task of self-protection to the more beneficial task of asserting the self's valid needs. It becomes easier for the self to promote its own causes, as it emotionally acknowledges its own worth, as well as the worth of what it has to offer in trade.

As the child within matures, the split-off parts of the personality become integrated into a new whole. The wound left by inadequate parenting many years ago heals as the individual finds more acceptable ways of stating personal needs, handling disappointment, and channeling aggressive energies. The futile efforts of the false self to satisfy needs by attracting attention and admiration can be released.

Knowing that you can withstand a negative situation releases the fear of failure. It allows you to move on and accept the challenges facing you. Trust in yourself grows as you experience your ability to overcome negatives and resistance.

An emotionally mature person recognizes more than black-and-white solutions. She realizes that a decision does not have to be perfect—and can never be perfect in the real world—in order to put her emotional energies fully behind it. A decision is not a means of magically resolving the manifold and contradictory forces impinging on us, nor of fulfilling grandiose dreams while remaining totally safe and invulnerable. We are called upon to decide amid—and in spite of—external resistance, conflicting goals, uncertainty, and confusion.

**A decision does not have to be perfect
in order for you to put your energy
fully behind it.**

MAKE AFFIRMATIONS THAT WORK FOR YOU

> Denying myself seems easy and natural. *Affirming* myself
> is scary, for it means I must say—at least to myself—who
> I am, what I want, and what I value. I cannot do this without
> leaving my safe cloak of invisibility. As soon as I affirm
> these things, others may hurt me, reject me, and ridicule
> me.

It's not easy to find people who can affirm us. Genuine
affirmation is a very scarce commodity. Most people feel diminished if they hand out too many good strokes or sincere
compliments. Although obtaining affirmation and emotional
nourishment from other people is important, you often have little
control over when and how this occurs. For this reason, I think
affirmations are extremely important, especially to decision makers who are treading on new ground. With affirmations, you can
"hear" the specific kinds of encouragement that help you sustain
your chosen course of action.

You *must* develop some form of positive self-talk to overcome the losses, failures, insults, and injustices that are inevitably
encountered in any sustained course of action. You must become
your own cheering section. Without positive self-talk, the negatives will slowly erode your confidence and vitality.

An *affirmation* is a positive statement that acknowledges
the worth of your self, your goals, your resources, and your
abilities. Significantly, an affirmation uses the present tense. It
acknowledges your worth and goals *today,* not sometime in the
future when other people may (or may not) be able to value you
similarly. Affirmation recognizes the fact that *now* possesses
more power and leverage than tomorrow.

Genuine affirmation is a very scarce commodity.

Each time you affirm your worth, ability, values, and trust
in your own judgment—you sustain and refuel vital emotional
energies. At first, you may feel a little silly affirming such things
to yourself. Why pat yourself on the back when nobody else

sees you this way or offers similar encouragement? Yet, if *you* don't do it, who should? It's within your power. Moreover, it's your responsibility to provide yourself with adequate support, even if it's from yourself.

Most successful people use positive self-talk, in one form or another. They also understand the necessity for doing it regularly. Especially when beginning a venture, they use affirmation to remind themselves of their goals and their desire to meet them.

Affirm your goals frequently. The process of developing a positive attitude toward yourself is one of reinforcement. What you surround yourself with, grows. When you stop practicing the positive feedback of affirmation, the negative springs right back up in its place. We are accustomed to thinking in terms of problems, things that are going *wrong*, not things that are going *right*.

Affirmations are assertions that certain things are right this very moment. They acknowledge the strength we can draw from those aspects of our being that are powerful and focused toward making us fulfilled and happy. It is a refreshing change to the constant flood of negativity to which we are exposed. The news is full of reports of murders, wars, earthquakes, deaths, betrayals, scandals, and scores of other miseries. The world abounds with people who have been defeated by life, people who have settled too easily, people who are frustrated. These negatives certainly exist. Yet, the world itself is neither negative nor positive. We need to acknowledge the positive and our power to actualize it in our own lives. Constantly remember your goal and your desires!

Affirmations are assertions that certain things are right this very moment.

AFFIRMATIONS REALLY WORK

From 1989 to 1991 I was a visiting professor at the University of Massachusetts. When I accepted the position, I had never taught before. I had no idea whether I could teach, but only a strong desire to try it and see.

Each day I went to school, I made an affirmation: *I am giving my very best effort to teaching today.* I committed my wits, time, and energy to learning how to teach well.

I discovered many things that helped: leveling with students, talking face to face, using visual aids, presenting interesting examples and historical developments, and most of all, posing a problem and asking the students how *they* would solve it. I prodded them to use the knowledge and common sense they already had and extend it to a new situation.

My techniques must have been successful, for the students in my department chose me for their "Professor of the Year" award. It was the first time a visiting professor had ever won such an award. At the annual awards dinner, I had the overwhelming experience of being given a standing ovation by two hundred students and faculty. I shall never forget that! It was living proof that affirmations can have very powerful results.

Affirmations should be stated in positive form. "I choose to fill my life with fulfilling relationships" is better than "I intend to avoid destructive relationships." Further, you must believe it is within your power to make your affirmations manifest. If not, revise them into statements that you *do* believe you can actualize. No one else has to believe them, only you!

Affirmations that are not properly qualified can do more harm than good. If they claim too much, they falsely pump up your ego and foster unrealistic expectations. For example, the affirmations "I am the *best* athlete" and "I deserve love from *everyone* I meet" will set you up for a fall. When you suffer the setback, you'll be forced to deny either your experience or the affirmation. Some people actually choose to deny what happened rather than give up an inflated self-image. Others dismiss affirmations as being ineffective. They conclude that affirmations are just wishful thinking. It's essential, therefore, to qualify your affirmations. Better versions of these affirmations are, "I am a good athlete" and "I deserve love."

Proper affirmations can guide you toward greater self-esteem. They do not feed the grandiose self that insists it can do *anything*. The shadow side of such overconfidence is a split-off "bad self" that feels totally helpless and unworthy. Instead, find the middle ground. Assert and affirm your right and ability to do *some* of the things you want and need.

Courage is an important quality in making affirmations. It takes guts to say who you are and what you value. Courage helps in making affirmations because it is difficult to *prove* them. Others, if they hear your affirmations, may disagree or counter with different views.[2] Many people are their own worst critic in this regard and are skeptical of affirmations altogether. It takes courage to postpone judgment about the benefit of affirmations until you have experienced the results.

Some sample affirmations are given on the next page. Use those that are powerful and relevant for you. I encourage you to develop additional ones that apply to your situation. Write them down and carry them in your wallet, or place them on your bureau where you can glance at them every day.

---

[2] It is not necessary to tell others of your affirmations. If they work, others will be seeing the *results*.

AFFIRMATIONS

> In choosing, I tell the world what kind of a person I am. In affirming, I tell myself.

I respect myself.

My decisions reflect my desire for fulfillment.

I am interesting, talented, and lovable. Certain other people see me that way, too!

I have the courage to take first steps toward my goals.

My resourcefulness helps me overcome obstacles.

I am honest with myself in seeing whether an experiment is working.

I deserve love.

I am the pivot of power in my own life.

I handle my fears well.

My ability to tolerate criticism from others is improving.

I am accepting the things I can't change.

I choose to fill my life with positive relationships.

I am willing to try in order to gain more experience.

I support and encourage those who are dear to me.

I am strong enough to endure setbacks.

I am planning for my success.

I prepare and practice for best results.

I refresh myself with wholesome recreation.

I honor my body with a healthy diet, adequate sleep, and good exercise.

I am patient for results to appear.

My feelings are an important part of me.

My ideas and help are useful to others.

I am learning to trust my own judgment.

I deserve to have interesting work and job satisfaction.

12

BALANCE YOUR EFFORTS

DON'T PUT ALL YOUR EGGS
IN ONE BASKET

Our society offers us a great deal of freedom to choose personal life-styles. In fact, never in the history of humankind have people had such a wide range of options available. This freedom of choice is a mixed blessing. Because there are so few restrictions, nothing holds us back from devoting all our energy to just one aspect of our lives. We can pursue that single aspect with greater intensity than would be possible otherwise and gain the corresponding rewards. What is not immediately apparent is that pursuing one aspect solely—to the near exclusion of all others—results in a profound sense of misproportion.

175

Pouring all our emotional energy into a single watertight compartment makes us lose sight of the larger dimensions of human existence.

We meet life in seven primary contexts:

1. Work
2. Family
3. Social
4. Recreation
5. Financial
6. Health
7. Spiritual

If you put all your eggs in just one of these seven baskets, you may develop great skill, make many friends, or earn much money. But if this area of your life ever fails you, you'll have nowhere to go. Your world will seem to come crashing down around you. When the "self-esteem eggs" in that one basket are gone, you'll feel like a nothing. This sounds like insurance policy thinking, but it's not. People who have played this game both ways insist that there are positive reasons why balancing your life is a much better way to live.

Balancing your life among these seven contexts makes you a whole person. Balance makes you comfortable not just in a single context, but in *all* the contexts in which you live. It allows you to draw sustenance from these other contexts. When you're balanced, you can meet a wider range of decision challenges. You don't always have to play the single role in which you have put most of your energy. You're free to play the roles required by the situation.

A single goal or activity cannot nourish us in every context, so we must devote some time to satisfying the other contexts. Furthermore, balanced people do not expect a single context to provide benefits that should properly be satisfied within other contexts. They know they have a better chance of total satisfaction if they address needs within each individual context.

For example, if you have put all your energy into your business, you may wishfully think that business associates should also be attracted to you socially or romantically. Even if they experience you as powerful and amiable in a business context, however, they may not want to extend their positive regard in this way. Because social relationships are inherently different from business relationships, it would be more appropriate to develop a social life that addressed these separate needs. The resulting relationships would not be based on a business power hierarchy, but on mutual compatibility and affability.

Balancing is an inner process instead of an outer one. Although others may try to tell you how to balance "from the outside," the only one who can truly say when you are balanced is *you*. Balancing is an intuitive, feeling process that helps you access when something is missing or too prevalent in your life.

Balance is an essential part of decision making. When you make a decision that "zero budgets" most of the other aspects of your life, you're setting yourself up for eventual disaster. You might, indeed, obtain such a single-minded goal. As a person, though, you won't be happy with yourself. Chapter 10 stated, "You are not the experiment; if the experiment fails, *you* are not a failure." The converse is also true: If the experiment succeeds, *you* are not a success. In our society, which worships outward success, discovering this truth can be very disillusioning.

> **If your "experiment" succeeds,
> it doesn't necessarily mean that *you*
> are a success.**

Many outwardly successful people hide behind their success. They cannot bear to be seen in any other context. Single-minded pursuit of their goal causes them to become less dimensional as people, less able to relax, and less comfortable with themselves.

Sam was a neighbor of mine. Born to immigrant parents, he was the first person in his family to go to college. He started his own business—a high-rise construction company—at the age of thirty. Sam was an industrious and resourceful manager. He put in many extra hours and went to extremes to satisfy his customers. By the age of forty he became a multimillionaire and owned a leasing company and an engineering design firm as well.

Sam was liked and respected at work. He had a knack for recognizing good opportunities and capitalizing on them. He knew how to put together a good management team. He studied business trends in his field and used the latest technologies.

Sam died of a heart attack at age forty-eight. A few months after the funeral, his wife, Susan, told me, "Sam's death was neither hereditary nor accidental. Sam *killed* himself."

"Sam was working sixteen hours a day. He had no time for exercise. His diet did not receive the same careful attention as his building plans. Sam had no time for us. He thought relaxation was useless. He never took vacations or observed holidays. His life was work, work, work."

Susan continued, "Sam's success over the years did not change his personality. We bought a nicer house and fancier cars, but inside, Sam remained anxious. He was always struggling to become more successful. He couldn't take the time to smell the flowers or play."

With tears in her eyes, Susan told me, "Sam cheated himself. He cheated us. His wealth may have fooled you, but Sam did not know how to live."

FIND YOUR OWN BALANCE POINT

Balancing involves a natural flow between action and relaxation. In action, we impute ourselves into the game. We face risk and reward, victory and loss. In relaxation, we settle back and give ourselves time for contemplation, interpretation, redirection, and inner affirmation. The balanced person has a *center* from which he or she is able to move either way, into action or relaxation.

It's difficult to be active and relaxed at the same instant. Activity requires a certain amount of self-generated tension by which we thrust ourselves forward. Because our attention is centered outward on the action itself, there is usually little left over for inward focus and direction.

The ancient Chinese Taoist philosophy of *wu-wei* emphasizes the balance between the opposites of action and relaxation (nonaction). Developing a rhythm between push and rest results in *economy of effort*.

Developing a rhythm between push and rest results in *economy of effort*.

Without a certain degree of bodily and mental relaxation, effort (action) becomes wasteful. We have all had the experience of "trying too hard." We immersed ourselves in action to the point where we no longer appreciated or sensed whether our actions were having the desired effect. In a manner of speaking, when you try too hard, your brain becomes disconnected from your brawn. You are unable to utilize your intelligence properly. Trying too hard means that you are exhausting yourself in an effort that is futile. The effort should be modified or applied to a different situation.

The peacefulness of inaction balances the tensions generated by intense action. Without this rest, you would quickly burn out. Inactivity and recreation are the antidote. Relaxation allows you to rekindle your sense of purpose and direction.

Too much relaxation can be just as unbalancing as too much activity, though. Sometimes, we simply don't try hard enough. In particular, people with thin skins are very attracted to relaxation techniques. They overuse a valid interest in meditation, contemplation, and recreation to avoid facing the risks of focused action. They cannot generate the amount of inward and motivating tension to propel themselves dynamically into action. Such people must realize that they don't have to give up their meditation to become active again. All they must do is accept that they must spend *some* of their time in the world of action. Thin-skinned people must bear the inner tension during these times to obtain the results that they want. They need to appreciate the natural ebb and flow between action and nonaction.

When your efforts are balanced, it appears that a *principle of least action* is operating: The effort that produces the desired result is the minimum required. All excess effort tends to throw you off balance or is absorbed by the body in the form of muscular tension and headache. Insufficient effort leads to lazy habits, poor attention, and lack of will to apply yourself. Thus, balance involves just the right amount of tension: not too much, not too little.

One important way balance is achieved is to give yourself time to unwind after an unusually intense "game" has been completed or played out. No matter whether the game has taken an hour or five years, we all need time to:

- Recover and absorb the changes
- Meditate over our actions and discover how we feel about them
- Assess our intuitive reactions to the experiences (dreams, insights, and hunches)
- Visualize how the next part of the game can be played

Be gentle to yourself. Don't push too hard when you should be unwinding. In particular, after a significant failure, loss, or injury, don't immediately bury yourself in action to distract yourself from the pain you are feeling. Lie fallow, feel the pain, and then move on with greater direction and purpose. For that matter, even victories should be treated this way. They, too, need to be balanced with relaxation and inactivity to prepare for the next game.

ORIENT YOURSELF TOWARD GROWTH

Good decisions support personal growth. But what is personal growth? It's the evolution you make through your life, as you mold it to both outside conditions and inner values. Bad decisions ignore the direction of your inner evolution or misapprehend vital outside conditions and consequences.

Although good decisions are extremely important to personal growth, it's unnecessary to maintain a tense "do-or-die" attitude about them. Here is an important truth about decisions that will make it much easier to relax with them: *A single decision will rarely make you or break you.* Ultimate success doesn't depend on isolated decisions made in moments of grand inspiration, but rather on the ability to support or change basic decisions as time goes by.

Successful people often make unsuccessful choices, but then they refine and revise these choices to better approach their goals. They *redecide*, based on current reality. Good decisions give full attention to new events and situations and do not obscure the present with memories of "what once was" or fantasies of "what might have been."

What appears to be a single major decision is actually a group of smaller subdecisions already in place. The larger decisions effectively *integrate* the smaller ones to make a single course of action more intelligible to ourselves and others.

The practical significance of this integrating principle is enormous. It says we should pay close attention to our values and motives at each step in the decision process. For in the long run, we cannot decide "against our values" without paying a huge price: We *dis*integrate the constellation of values and intentions that forms our very self, resulting in profound anxiety.

In the long run, you cannot decide "against your values" without paying a huge price.

Looking at the smaller decisions in ensemble allows us to see—often for the first time—that we've been trying to *reverse* a major decision made many years ago. Norman, for example, was an accountant who wanted to be an artist. For many years, he considered his situation and desire, but always "decided" against art as a career. He never paid much attention to what the smaller decisions in his life were telling him:

- Leaving a series of accounting jobs out of a vague feeling of dissatisfaction
- Not keeping up with professional developments in accounting
- Avoiding going the extra mile in his accounting work
- Sketching at lunch break everyday
- Exhibiting in the community art show for five years in a row
- Having sold 65 paintings for a total of $33,000 in the past four years
- Seeking out and forming friendships with artists
- Taking advanced art courses to improve his skills

When it was pointed out to Norman that these smaller decisions, taken as a whole, had a very strong message, he was able to reconsider his "big" decision with more confidence and appreciation for his values.

The study of entrepreneurs in business sheds further light on the relationship between decision-making ability and success. Entrepreneurs are not afraid to make high-risk decisions. Their commitment is not to consistency, but to changing the experiment (and therefore, the decision) until a positive result is found. They regard decisions with far less finality than most of us.

The entrepreneur makes some good decisions and some bad ones, but does not feel obliged to stick with obviously poor decisions (consistency for the sake of consistency). The entrepreneur's hunger for success overcomes the anxiety of constantly having to change the experiment.

> ## The entrepreneur's desire for success overcomes the anxiety of constantly having to change the experiment.

Successful entrepreneurs typically try half a dozen ventures before one of them catches on. That is, their decision-making batting average is about .200. With a new venture, there is no cookbook recipe to make great decisions every time. Nobody knows until the experiment is tried. The only way to get results is to evaluate decisions after they have been made and redecide whether to continue, abort, or try harder.

Entrepreneurs are a special group of people who are attracted to high-risk, high-payoff situations. One reason even successful entrepreneurs appear to have such a low batting average is that their goals and values preclude exactly those average-risk, average-payoff situations that form the bulk of decision-making scenarios.

The rest of us can profit from the entrepreneurial attitude, even if we embrace less ambitious goals. Our situation is not really different:

Axiom: Five out of ten choices will not work out at all, even if they are made with great decision skill. Of the remaining five, three will require major modification or sacrifice to be made workable. One will work with minor modification. This leaves only one out of the ten that will work without any further effort.

Corollary: Choosing is risky. The riskier your plans, the more frequently you should monitor them.

TAKE RESPONSIBILITY FOR YOUR OWN LIFE

It's no accident that certain people wind up in their particular situation. They gravitate to it by virtue of their personality. These people *try* to change and *try* to decide wisely. However, when they choose against their fate, they experience losing more often than winning. Or, they run out of "emotional gas" in pursuing their new choices. They scurry back to safe strategies that work and give up in an essential way. They restructure subsequent choices to avoid further failure and humiliation. They close themselves off from new choices and lose the will to experiment.

Many of us are reluctant to experiment, even when we can do it safely and without subsequent commitment. Why? We're afraid of what the answer might be. If the experiment's results are positive, we would then lack our excuse for not acting on it. We keep ourselves deliberately ignorant to ward off the anxiety of having to act. I feel that there is a more useful attitude toward experimenting: Life measures you by what you do and who you are, not by what you do *not* do and who you are *not*.

Refusing to experiment means refusing to learn. This has great significance for decision makers, because *decision making is a learning process.* Learning and deciding are inseparable partners in the larger process of personal growth. Making decisions teaches you how to deal with change, risk, uncertainty, failure—and most important—how to become successful.

> ## Decision making is a learning process.

It's impossible to avoid important decisions without suffering dire consequences. In this context, there is a subtle difference between *refusing to decide* and *deciding to do nothing* about a situation. In the latter, after we have considered the problem, its relevance to us, and our personal responsibility for taking action, we may judge that our best option is to do nothing. We can ignore it, tolerate it, or delegate it to someone else. Perhaps it will go away after a short time. Perhaps we may address it when the conditions of the problem are different or if it becomes more urgent. Whatever the case, we decide not to accept the challenge posed by the situation at that moment.

Refusing to decide has the same external effect as deciding to do nothing, but the internal effect—on your emotions—is vastly different. Refusing to decide is neither accepting nor rejecting the challenge posed by the situation, but rejecting the responsibility to become the active agent in your own life.

Refusing to decide is, in itself, a decision. It is a decision to let events and external circumstances point the direction in your life. It is an act of alienation and self-exclusion. Consistently refusing to decide leads to an impoverished sense of self, to confusion, and to anger at the system for not guessing your needs and automatically providing them.

Refusing to decide is a form of emotional suicide. It destroys the inner self that provides purpose and direction. People who refuse to decide go through the motions, but have disconnected their will from their actions. They may become successful—accidentally—but not in the ways they *want* to become successful. Effective decision makers recognize when they are caught in the rut of refusing to decide and make every effort to climb out.

> ## Refusing to decide is a *decision* to let external circumstances direct your life.

APPRECIATE THE VALUE OF COMMITMENT

In conclusion, I'd like to leave you with some very good news. It's altogether possible to gain *clarity* in decision making. Clarity comes from appreciating the value of commitment and from seeing the *necessity* of making choices. Clarity helps you to face the large decisions in your life and make the choices that will most benefit you in the future.

Commitment to a "course of thinking" is not sufficient in decision making. A decision is a commitment to a course of *action*. When you're committed to action, you enter the realm of risk. Thoughts—which are a very important component of decisions—do not, by themselves, commit you in the same way. Thoughts can't provide the emotional energy, work, and sacrifice to assure that you'll arrive at the goal.

Because commitment is so valuable, we have to limit ourselves and be wise in the many commitments we make everyday. We can do only so much, and must recognize our limitations to best achieve our goals.

Heraclitus suggested that life is a balance of opposites in tension. The whole person manages to integrate these opposites in a way that allows him or her to move on. Power, knowledge, and capability come from acting in spite of the many opposites that pull at the separate parts of our consciousness. It is perhaps ironic that clarity emerges from nonclarity, from living with the paradoxes:

- We are separate and, yet, somehow connected.
- Good would not exist without evil.
- Humility grows out of deep self-love.
- The long way is often the short way.
- Trying (too hard) can be a form of nontrying.
- Commitment requires a certain kind of detachment.

Clarity helps us appreciate the contradictions in our actions—without guilt, anxiety, or fear—and simply move on. The contradictions can never be totally eliminated. There are no *simple* answers. Forcing things into black-and-white categories only generates troublesome emotions. Accepting the contradictions means you understand yourself as a perfectly worthy person who makes imperfect actions (sometimes) in a (usually) imperfect world.

Embracing the paradoxes brings a great sense of relief. You don't need to justify your actions with absolute precision. You don't need to hold yourself hostage to previous errors or choices. You can simply act to the best of your knowledge and intention today.

EPILOGUE

The twelve methods presented in *Decision Power* can work for you. They form the building blocks of good decision making. Some of the methods sharpen the processes of your rational mind. Others help you access your feelings and values so that they can be factored into the decision. The remaining methods promote strength, resourcefulness, and resilience. Taken as a group, they can cut your big decisions down to size.

The twelve methods work in concert. To see this, let's consider how you—the decision maker—interact with the environment to get the things you need. A decision problem means that there is something that you need. A decision solution means that you have successfully extracted (traded) that something from the environment.

The accompanying figure, "How the Twelve Methods Fit Together," shows this unique view of the decision-making process. It portrays three *arenas* (represented by circles) in which a decision maker is involved: Resources & Skills, Self, and Environment.

How the Twelve Methods Fit Together

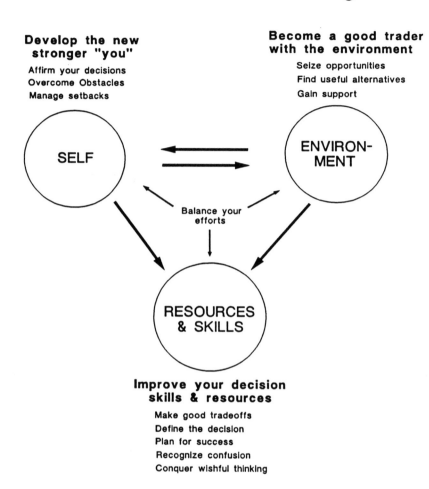

Develop the new stronger "you"

Affirm your decisions
Overcome Obstacles
Manage setbacks

Become a good trader with the environment

Seize opportunities
Find useful alternatives
Gain support

SELF

ENVIRON-MENT

Balance your efforts

RESOURCES & SKILLS

Improve your decision skills & resources

Make good tradeoffs
Define the decision
Plan for success
Recognize confusion
Conquer wishful thinking

The first arena, *Resources & Skills*, is placed beneath the other two. Resources and skills are like the roots of a tree. They provide the support upon which the visible part of the tree depends. Resources are things you have already obtained from the environment. They are under your control. You can store them and call upon them when you require them. Improving your resources makes you more capable of carrying out your decisions.

Skills are grouped with resources because once gained, they form part of a reservoir that can be tapped on demand. One skill in particular—learning to plan—should be singled out with respect to resources. Planning is extremely valuable because it is, in essence, *managing* resources. Planning allows you to best use the resources already in your command and helps you obtain the additional resources needed to reach your goals. Four other skills that form part of every decision maker's repertoire are defining the decision, making good trade-offs, recognizing confusion, and conquering wishful thinking.

The second arena, *Self*, focuses on developing the new stronger "you." Strengthening your self means becoming more capable, more empowered, and more confident. It results in higher self-esteem, increased self-awareness, and greater ability to bounce back from negative events. You will come to know that you are worth the efforts required to fulfill your needs, instead of letting them go unaddressed and feeling less of a person. The methods used in this arena are overcoming obstacles, managing setbacks, and affirming your self.

The third arena, *Environment*, is where you learn to become a good trader. Good traders know how to seize opportunities and find useful alternatives. They perceive the decision scenario and context realistically. They have learned to stay informed about important changes occurring in the world. This way, they are sure that they always have something of value to offer for the things that will fulfill their needs. Finally, good traders know how to gain support from the environment by networking, including loved ones in their decisions, and getting useful advice from others.

The only method that resists classification is *balance your efforts*. This method transcends the three arenas. It provides the glue that keeps the enterprise called "you" together. Balancing your efforts urges you to expend effort in all the important areas of your life, not just your favorite ones.

The connectedness of "How the Twelve Methods Fit Together" is striking. Everything hangs together. This is not to say that decision making must be complicated, but only that decision makers eventually learn to perform a variety of roles, including the rational scientist who conducts experiments, the feeling person who nurtures goals, the networker who builds support, the trader who spots good deals, the judge who understands trade-offs, the strategist who develops plans and schedules, the minister who affirms self-worth, and the reporter who gathers facts and assesses situations.

Most of us have considerable experience in these roles. In helping others make decisions, I have found that most adults are adequate decision makers—in a general sense. When challenged by a particular important decision, however, many people are able to make major improvements by focusing on just one or two areas they have neglected. All that is required is a nudge in the right direction. These suggestions, which vary from person to person, include, for example,

- Make a better plan
- Be more aggressive (or less aggressive)
- Get more information
- Don't give up (or don't hang on)
- Seek more appropriate opportunities
- Do an experiment to find out

Therefore, please don't think that you must be an expert in all this book's methods to make good decisions. If you carry away only one or two new ideas to try in your own decision process, my aim in writing this guide will have been fulfilled.

Allow yourself the time to grow as a decision maker. Developing strength takes practice and experience. It's like weight lifting. You can't become an accomplished weight lifter overnight. True, you can momentarily exceed your abilities. Real growth, however, is based on the ability to do a particular exercise repeatedly, on demand, and *without damage* to your body. With coaching, weight lifters assess their weaknesses and devise strategies to improve on them. They practice daily, use proper tools, and slowly work up to greater goals. The way a healthy ego is built up in decision making is totally analogous.

Furthermore, each of us starts from a different spot. It is therefore appropriate to accept your unique situation, wherever you are. That is, decision making is not a race! It is a skill that embraces the very fabric of your life, helping give it more direction and fulfillment. Once you accept your current starting point, it's easier to make wiser and more fulfilling decisions.

With self-acceptance, decision making takes on a different character. The tendency to imitate or compete with others—who have different situations, resources, and values—vanishes. Self-acceptance allows you to move at your own speed and in your own way. I encourage you to access your wisdom, courage, and resourcefulness in this regard—and wish you the very best results from your decisions.

APPENDIX

EVALUATE THE QUALITY OF YOUR DECISION

This self-quiz will help you evaluate the quality of decisions you may be considering. There are no right or wrong answers. Instead of a score, the quiz provides a *checklist* for many of the issues treated in this book. It will make you aware of the need to go back and consider particular aspects more fully. Some questions may not pertain directly to your individual decision or situation. In this case, I encourage you to modify them accordingly and ask yourself questions that elucidate the real issues.

When it comes to personal decisions, the notion of *quality* is elusive. There are no objective standards, no quantitative scales, to measure exactly how good a decision is. What is a good decision for you may be a bad decision for me. What was a good decision for you yesterday may be a poor decision today.

One measure for the quality of decisions is the results. Yet, measuring decisions *solely* by results can lead to serious error. Sometimes, good decisions lead to bad outcomes; sometimes bad decisions lead to good outcomes.

One reason for this discrepancy is that many decisions are complicated by uncertainty. Sometimes, you must decide before you can gather all the necessary information. Sometimes, that information is not known or available. At other times, the effort required to gain the information may be more than you are willing or able to exert. Finally, unanticipated events outside your control can also influence the results strongly.

To account for uncertainty and wide differences in personal values and situations, it is wiser to judge decisions by the *process* used to arrive at them. *Decision Power's* twelve proven methods for cutting big decisions down to size helps you with exactly these processes: looking at both the rational and emotional aspects; defining the problem; adjusting for your biases; including your values; estimating the risks, rewards, and probable consequences; planning; and gaining support. The decision that emerges will not eliminate the uncertainties or negative situations, but it will allow you to move forward in spite of them.

IS THIS A *GOOD* DECISION?

1. Does the decision support or reflect my personal values?
2. Does it bring me closer to my goals?
3. Does it satisfy my basic needs?
4. Does it provide benefits for my time, energy, and effort?
5. Have I made a plan to sustain the chosen course?
6. Does it make good use of my time?
7. Does it anticipate the major obstacles along the way and consider how to overcome them?
8. Can I commit to it with my whole heart?
9. Does it bring me into contact with people who support my purposes?
10. Does it face the problem rather than run away from it?
11. Does it consider the relevant information?
12. Does it use my intelligence and creativity?
13. Does it improve my ability to weather setbacks and unforeseen changes? (That is, does it make my situation more stable?)
14. Does it lead to promising alternatives, or is it dead-ended?

15. Does it reflect a realistic assessment of my abilities, finances, and energies?
16. Did I consider *all* my alternatives?
17. Was I realistic in evaluating the feasibility of my options?

IS THIS A *BAD* DECISION?

1. Have I made the decision in anger or emotional upset?
2. Have I ignored the commitments that will be required?
3. Did I fool myself about the real issues?
4. Has wishful thinking allowed me to misjudge the situation?
5. Have I neglected to anticipate possible resistance from others?
6. Have I been unwilling to admit that I really wanted something else?
7. Am I choosing the path of least resistance, when something harder is appropriate?
8. Have I denied myself the effort to discover and formulate more worthwhile goals?
9. Have I overlooked or prematurely dismissed significant alternatives?
10. Have I avoided planning?
11. Did I postpone the decision until the matter was decided *for* me?
12. Was I unwilling to *back* the decision with the required effort and resources?
13. Do I regret the opportunities lost in choosing the current option?
14. Have I ignored basic *needs* in pursuing my *wants*?
15. Did I deliberately seek out biased advice?
16. Did I neglect to obtain sufficient information about the alternatives?
17. Did I use *all-or-nothing* thinking to generate my alternatives?
18. Did I let anxiety keep me stuck, constantly rechecking my bad situation?

SUGGESTED READING
LIST

ALBRECHT, KARL, *Successful Management by Objectives.*
Englewood Cliffs, NJ: Prentice Hall, 1978.

> *Management by Objectives* has a simple philosophy: Most people work
> better when they know what the goals are, when they are motivated to
> accept these goals, and when they anticipate getting rewarded for helping
> achieve them. Many of the business MBO principles Karl Albrecht de-
> scribes are applicable to decision making in general. His discussions of
> goal setting, organizing complex work tasks, and avoiding the activity
> trap are excellent.

BALLAS, GEORGE C., AND DAVID HOLLAS, *The Making of an Entrepreneur.* Englewood Cliffs, NJ: Prentice Hall, 1980.

> "The most important element in determining the success of a new business
> is the entrepreneur." Such are one of the many "guidelines on how to
> think and behave entrepreneurially" given in this punchy and colorful
> book by the inventor of the Weed Eater. Ballas's attitude toward success
> supports the principle given in Chapter 12 of *Decision Power*: "Change
> the experiment until it works."

BEHN, ROBERT D., AND JAMES W. VAUPEL, *Quick Analysis for Busy Decision Makers*. New York: Basic Books, 1982.

> Behn and Vaupel offer a shortcut method for making personal, business, and governmental decisions when "time is short and information is limited." They explain (with detailed examples) how to simplify decisions, how to assess risk, how to deal with uncertainty, and how to make trade-offs. Their method makes extensive use of decision trees and will appeal to anyone with a mathematical bent. This book is not exactly light reading, but it offers rewarding insights if you're willing to put in the effort.

BURKA, JANE B., AND LENORA M. YUEN, *Procrastination*. Reading, MA: Addison-Wesley, 1983.

> Burka and Yuen offer a readable and engaging discussion of procrastination and its many faces. They analyze *why* we put things off and describe the many psychological mechanisms we use to justify inaction. Finally, the book gives an entire program for managing procrastination.

DE BONO, EDWARD, *Tactics*. Boston: Little, Brown, 1984.

> Edward de Bono, the renowned expert on creative thinking, examines the tactics used by successful people throughout history. He discusses many issues of interest to decision makers, such as, Should you create opportunities or seek them out? Do you need to take risks to succeed? When should you listen to your intuition? How rigid should a strategy be? How far is success in your control? How should you interpret your strengths and weaknesses?

GILBREATH, ROBERT D., *Forward Thinking*. New York: McGraw-Hill, 1987.

> This book is an insightful discussion of *change*, written mainly for corporate managers. It offers advice on how to recognize change, how to respond to it, how to prepare for it, and how to integrate it into your business style. I found the chapter on the dangers of overspecialization unique and illuminating. Highly recommended.

HAMILTON, N. GREGORY, *Self and Others*. Northvale, NJ: Jason Aronson, 1988.

> The most significant psychotherapeutic advance in the past thirty years is object relations theory. Hamilton's survey of this new field is lucid, readable, and comprehensive. It shows how "good enough" nurturing in infancy results in a strong self capable of trading effectively with the outside world.

HYATT, CAROLE, AND LINDA GOTTLIEB, *When Smart People Fail.*
New York: Simon & Schuster, 1987.

> The authors interviewed almost two hundred "smart people" who failed
> and then rebounded to greater success. The result is this inspiring book,
> which is a testament to people's ability to survive and overcome disaster.
> The book offers many useful suggestions on how to *reinvent* yourself
> after a setback.

JANIS, IRVING L., AND LEON MANN, *Decision Making.*
New York: The Free Press, 1977.

> This classic study is subtitled, "A Psychological Analysis of Conflict,
> Choice, and Commitment." It explores the psychological processes behind
> decision making and offers ways to improve them. Janis and Mann's
> style is more academic than most of the books in this reading list, but
> the material is very useful nevertheless.

JOHNSON, STEPHEN M., *Humanizing the Narcissistic Style.*
New York: W. W. Norton, 1987.

> Although this down-to-earth book is written primarily for psychothera-
> pists, *anybody* can derive benefit from it. Johnson's explanation of nar-
> cissistic personality disorders and their cure is clear and jargon-free. This
> material will be of special interest to decision makers who were frustrated,
> deprived, or abused in their childhood.

KALELLIS, PETER M., *On the Other Hand . . . .*
Allen, TX: Argus Communications, 1980.

> The subtitle of this short book is "Deciding What to Do About Indecision."
> It is a gentle introduction to the spiritual dimensions of decision making.
> Kalellis portrays "the human paradox" as having to choose, even if none
> of the options is completely good or bad. Every option we choose will
> have some faults, and every option we forgo will have some merit. There-
> fore, we need to deal with ambivalence, uncertainty, and the pain of
> trade-offs. Kalellis offers good advice on accessing your inner strength
> to overcome procrastination and live decisively.

KARRASS, CHESTER L., *The Negotiating Game.*
New York: Thomas Y. Crowell, 1970.

> This well-written book covers the essentials of negotiating. Karrass offers
> a perspective that is especially appropriate to decision making. He has
> interesting discussions of tactics, strategy, how to be persuasive, the art
> of compromise, the role of status and power ("Status acts as a social
> guillotine among men. I have noticed over the years that layoffs in industry

rarely affect those on top . . ." p. 100), and the hidden dimensions of the negotiating process, such as nonverbal communication.

KAYE, HARVEY, *Inside the Technical Consulting Business.*
New York: John Wiley, 1986.

> This book is for technical specialists who are considering a switch from direct employment to consulting. In this specific context, it is a decision guide that discusses the necessary elements of a major career change: information gathering, assessing the market, making contacts, planning, selling your services, and dealing with clients.

KEPNER, CHARLES H., AND BENJAMIN B.TREGOE, *The New Rational Manager.* Princeton, NJ: Princeton Research Press, 1981.

> Kepner and Tregoe were the first to emphasize the importance of evaluating criteria from a dual perspective: the "must-haves" versus the "wants." Their book is a clear exposition of business decision making using *rational* means of problem definition and solution. Their method largely ignores the psychological dimensions of decision making (which may be entirely appropriate in many business situations).

MAY, ROLLO, *The Meaning of Anxiety,* rev. ed.
New York: W. W. Norton, 1977.

> Rollo May's classic survey of anxiety looks at the subject from three viewpoints: philosophy, psychology, and the history of anxiety theories. Although it is more difficult and specialized than most of the other books on this list, the effort to digest it will be rewarded with many insights. As I read it, I found myself underlining many sentences and marking entire paragraphs with double asterisks (my notation for "right on!").

PERLS, FRITZ, *The Gestalt Approach.*
Ben Lomond, CA: Science and Behavior Books, 1973.

> "For the individual to satisfy his needs . . . he must be able to sense *what* he needs and he must know *how* to manipulate himself and his environment, for . . . needs can only be satisfied through the *interaction* of the organism and the environment" (my emphasis). I highly recommend this short explanation of Gestalt therapy. Perls developed many of the concepts used in Chapter 7 of *Decision Power:* self, environment, contact (with the environment), the importance of self-other boundaries, accessing feelings here and now, and learning not to interrupt yourself from fulfilling your needs.

RICOEUR, PAUL, *Freedom and Nature.*
Evanston, IL: Northwestern University Press, 1966.

> French philosopher Paul Ricoeur offers a brilliant exposition of the decision process from a phenomenological viewpoint. Like most modern French philosophy, this book makes extreme demands on the reader's intellect, but rewards the effort with nuggets of wisdom and insights unavailable elsewhere. If you are intellectually inclined, this is great reading!

RUBIN, THEODORE I., *Compassion and Self-Hate.*
New York: David McKay, 1975.

> "He didn't realize for a long time that he had been using shifting goals as a key process in his behavior for years. This was the prime method he used to drive himself on and away from himself, and away from the possibility of giving himself decent, human satisfaction." (p. 125) If you have ever experienced self-defeating behavior in your life, or been deprived as a child, or discovered that you are sensitive to criticism, or felt you must do a perfect job—this book is a must read! It is a well-written, upbeat, and compassionate approach to enhancing self-esteem.

SIU, R. G. H., *The Craft of Power.*
New York: John Wiley, 1979.

> This book is a witty and philosophical guide to acquiring personal power. Siu is a modern Machiavelli whose conceptual views on tactics, strategies, and politics can be readily applied to decision making.

STEINER, GEORGE A., *Strategic Planning.*
New York: The Free Press, 1979.

> *Strategic Planning* is a step-by-step guide to the planning process. Although Steiner's viewpoint is more business oriented and formal than required for personal decisions, he covers all the major aspects of good planning: situation auditing, developing goals, formulating strategies, translating strategic plans into current decisions, and contingency planning.

VISCOTT, DAVID, *Risking.*
New York: Simon & Schuster, 1977.

> This popular best-seller is about learning how to take risks. Dr. Viscott's psychological approach is engaging, punchy, and provocative. Be it in the area of love, family, work, or personal growth, the book encourages you to take risks *appropriately.* Viscott gives you the tools to judge: When is this risk reasonable? When should I pass? When should I go for broke?

WILLIAMS, ANDREA, *Making Decisions.*
New York: Kensington Publishing, 1985.

> Williams has developed an interesting method for personal decision making that graphically displays the advantages and disadvantages of any two competing options. She then shows how to reduce the complex diagram to one of a group of general cases, to which she has given catchy names such as Tiger 'Neath the Tree, Monkey Bottles, and Cat's Cradle. Williams's method is especially good for trade-off issues, but may not be appropriate in more general decisions.

WURMAN, RICHARD SAUL, *Information Anxiety.*
New York: Doubleday, 1989.

> This is a fascinating and provocative study about the worldwide glut of information and our inability to digest it. Our society is more information rich than ever before, but, ironically, we still feel anxious about not knowing "enough." This book is the antidote. It encourages you, in a humorous way, to stop collecting data and start assembling knowledge.

INDEX